LET YAHSHUA ROCK YOUR WORLD

Murline Miles

Messiah's Truth
Allen, Texas

"Listen to Me, you who pursue righteousness, seeking Yahweh: Look to the ROCK you were hewn from, and to the hole of the pit you were dug from."
(Isaiah 51:1)

"There is no one Set-Apart (Holy) like Yahweh, for there is no one besides You, and there is no ROCK like our Elohim (Mighty One—God)."
(1 Samuel 2:2)

"The ROCK, His work is perfect, for all His ways are justice…"
(Deuteronomy 32:4)

"…and all drank the same spiritual drink. For they drank of that spiritual ROCK that followed, and the ROCK was Messiah."
(1 Corinthians 10:4)

LET YAHSHUA ROCK YOUR WORLD
© 2009 by Murline Miles

Published by Messiah's Truth
325 S. Jupiter Rd.
Suite 112
Allen, Texas 75002

All Rights Reserved
Printed in the United States of America

All Scriptures from "The Scriptures" version unless otherwise noted. Institute for Scripture Research. (PTY) Ltd Copyright © 1998. (www.messianic.co.za)

Correspond with the author at: mail@messiahstruth.com

Cover Concept by Craig Miles

Cover Design / Artwork by Kris Rogers

Edited by Eddie and Gayle Rogers

Dear Reader,

There is a sense in the atmosphere that something major could possibly be on the horizon in the not too distant future. Everywhere you turn there is news about things heating up in this world like never before. These warnings are coming from prophecy teachers as well as secular sources.

Psalm 91 starts out with, "He who dwells in the secret place of the Most High, Who abides under the shadow of the Almighty" then the next two verses continue to reveal that He is our refuge and our fortress and that He'll deliver us from the snare of the fowler and from pestilence. Verse 4 reads, "He covers you with His feathers, And under His wings you take refuge; His truth is a shield and amour."

That last sentence shows that we will trust under His "<u>wings</u>" and His "<u>truth</u>" shall be our shield. If asked, most believers would say they know His truth but perhaps would not know what's meant by His "wings." Well I discovered after 27 years in the faith, that I knew neither His truth nor His wings, although both will be crucial in these last days.

If you are a truth lover and you eagerly desire to know the truth and please your Creator, you'll find that this book will help you along that path. You'll learn what it means to abide in Him and what really pleases Him. He gives us the answers in His Word, but most have been blinded because of indoctrination into the traditions of men.

"Let Yahweh Rock Your World" with His Truth,

Murline

> "Yahweh is my Rock and my Stronghold and my Deliverer; My Ěl (Mighty One) is my Rock, I take refuge in Him…"
> (Psalm 18:2)

Table of Contents

INTRODUCTION: Hidden Things Are Being Revealed — 9

Chapter 1: If I Were The Enemy — 15

Chapter 2: Idioms — 27

Chapter 3: What's In A Name? — 45

Chapter 4: Sabbath — 59

Chapter 5: It's The Law — 79

Chapter 6: Idols, Idols Everywhere! — 97

Chapter 7: Conclusion — 123

Appendix 1: Hebrew Idioms — 137

Appendix 2: Sabbath to Sunday — 167

Appendix 3: The Disciples Kept the Sabbath — 177

Appendix 4: Old Covenant Found in the New Covenant — 187

Appendix 5: Sabbath Around the World — 189

Appendix 6: GRACE — 197

Resources — 215

Questions and Answers — 221

> *"Guard me as the apple of Your eye. Hide me under the shadow of Your wings…"*
> *(Psalm 17:8)*

INTRODUCTION: Hidden Things Are Being Revealed

Like tens of thousands of others, I'm finding that what I <u>know</u> just isn't <u>so</u>.

Some things have been sealed up for the "end" and are now being revealed and more will be revealed as we get closer to the *end* of the end of days. Other truths have been revealed and are right out in the open, but the enemy has blinded our eyes with a "Western" mindset. Still other truths can only be discerned by getting familiar with the culture and the language of the Bible.

Those who love the Truth (He is the Way, the TRUTH and the Life) will have ears to hear what the Spirit is saying in these last days. They will return to their First Love, even if what they hear is 180 degrees opposite of what they've been taught all their lives.

Before you read any further, I suggest you pause and pray with a sincere heart to receive truth and then fasten your spiritual seatbelts because we're getting ready to go on what might be the ride of your lifetime. That's right, stop right now and pray. "Show

Let Yahshua Rock Your World

me Your ways, O Yahweh; Teach me Your paths. Lead me in Your truth and teach me, For You are the Elohim of my deliverance; On You I wait all the day" (Psalm 25:4-5).

For some, the concepts in this book will be like "shock" and "awe" *(that's how it was for me)*. But if these truths resonate in your spirit, I encourage you to swallow your pride, kick your ego to the curb and search the Scriptures for yourself to see whether these things are so.

Through years of reading and studying the Bible, there were many times when questions would pop into my mind that I just couldn't answer. And when I'd ask someone like a pastor or Bible teacher what certain Scripture verses meant, they'd respond with what seemed to be pat answers. At other times, I'd hear different pastors and teachers give several different interpretations of the same passage of Scripture.

Needless to say, it became frustrating so I found myself just skipping over those portions of Scripture and pushing the questions onto the back burner in my mind. Sometimes I even thought I was losing my mind because I just couldn't make any sense out of what I was reading.

But the Father had mercy and led me into studying the "Hebraic Roots" of the Christian faith. One day, while I was reading the Scriptures a verse seemed to leap off the page. It was Jeremiah 33:3 which says, 'Call unto Me, and I shall answer you, and show you great and inaccessible *matters*, which you have not

Hidden Things Are Being Revealed

known.' Indeed, these past few years have been like sitting under a fire hose.

He has revealed more truth to me in just the last two years alone than in all the twenty-seven years combined since I received salvation. It has been a phenomenal journey into His Word. The more I learn, the more I realize I don't know. I feel like I've only started to scratch a tiny part of the surface.

My desire is to provoke you to search the Scriptures for yourself and study with a Hebraic mindset rather than a Western, Greco-Roman mindset, because there is much buried treasure in the Hebrew culture and language that has been *lost in translation*.

When these ROCKS of revelation are unearthed, the Word of Truth will explode in your spirit like it did in mine. Joy unspeakable and full of glory will take on a whole new meaning. No longer will it be just some worked up emotional state of mind. You will have *hard evidence* of what pleases Him and you will know beyond the shadow of a doubt what it means to worship Him in Spirit and in Truth.

I know that the subjects covered in this book will ROCK your world, but I love you enough to risk offending you. Just remember His Word *never* appeals to the flesh, but it *always* appeals to the spirit. Therefore, the truths laid bare in this book may be extremely difficult to receive and may even cause emotional trauma because of strong indoctrination to the contrary. But rest assured that when you KNOW the Truth, the Truth will make you free (John 8:32).

Let Yahshua Rock Your World

My personal reaction to the things I'm sharing with you was first tears, then anger (that I had been deceived), and finally an overwhelming joy and thankfulness. But in the midst of the joy, my heart is heavy when I think about the millions of precious saints, who are being led astray.

The Father wants us to know Him and to be known by Him. I knew some of the things I'd seen in the Church and heard preached was "phony bologna macaroni," but for the most part I thought I was being taught how to know Him, serve Him, and please Him. I thought my faith was ROCK solid. But now I found that I was building on sand. It's impossible to please someone if you don't really know what they like and dislike, but you think you do. Here's an everyday life example of what I'm getting at:

> If I told my husband that I liked perfume *(because I'm really into fragrances)* and that's what I wanted him to buy me for special occasions; then that's what I would expect him to give me to demonstrate his love and his desire to please me. However, if he'd been conditioned to believe that flowers are what makes most women happy and he bought flowers instead of perfume (because they were not only pretty, but *they smelled good too*), I would perceive that he gave me what HE wanted to give me but not what I wanted.

Well the Creator, who made us, gave us a procedure manual (Bible) to live by that not only shows how much He loves us but it

Hidden Things Are Being Revealed

also shows us how to love and please Him. It's our responsibility to worship Him the way He wants to be worshipped – not according to some century's old false doctrines steeped in paganism. *(I hope that last sentence didn't make the hair stand up on the back of your neck.)*

When He convicts us of sin and reveals His TRUTHS to us, we have to be willing to repent and change regardless of what we've been taught in the past. There is nothing wrong with a man-made tradition as long as it meets two criteria: **1)** it does not go against the Word of Elohim and **2)** it is not purported to be the Word of Elohim.

However, there are many traditions of men in the "Church" today that disappoints and even angers our Savior because they are either *taught as His Word but are not in His Word,* or they are *condemned by His Word.*

If Paul or other first century disciples were to visit our churches today, they would no doubt wonder why "another gospel" is being preached and why there is so much pagan worship in the Church. Although there is nothing new under the sun, much has changed between the first century and the twenty-first century that would make the current day Gospel unrecognizable to them.

The Father is calling His people back to the old landmarks. He is looking for those who will offer to Him acceptable worship. He wants us to <u>hear</u> His Truths and <u>do</u> what He says to the best of our ability. So I'm inviting you to grab your shovel and come along with me and let's dig up some of His Truths from His Set-Apart (Holy) Written Word and build our house upon THE ROCK.

This book may be thought of as a beginner's guide for those desiring to return to the Hebrew roots of the Christian faith – a starting point if you will. My personal journey began when my husband prayed for His Truth, His whole Truth and nothing but His Truth. The next thing I knew we received an invitation from a friend to attend a Sukkot celebration and the rest is history as they say.

For deeper studies, there are several resources listed in the back of this book including website links and book titles from many wonderful, knowledgeable "Hebrew Roots" teachers that Yahweh has raised up for this hour.

I'm full of hope that *"LET YAHSHUA ROCK YOUR WORLD"* will first whet your appetite enough that you will desire to search out His Truths for yourself. Second, cause you to discern doctrines and teachings that are contrary to the Scriptures. And third, provoke you to return to your First Love and love Him the way He wants to be loved because HE IS WORTHY!

"And he said, 'Go, Dani'ĕl, for the words are hidden and sealed till the time of the end. Many shall be cleansed and made white, and refined. But the wrong shall do wrong – and none of the wrong shall understand, **but those who have insight shall understand**.'"
(Daniel 12:9-10)

… If I Were The Enemy

Chapter 1:
If I Were The Enemy

Using stealth of course, as the "enemy" of Elohim (GOD), I would cause the "Church" to fall into apostasy (fall away) by hiding the truth in plain view. Without even the slightest clue, *[although there are some who do have a clue, but choose to follow the status quo]* my methods would cause Christian leaders to fall into error by introducing doctrines of demons right under their noses.

From the very beginning, I would start adding to the Word of Elohim by planting an evil seed in Chavvah's (Eve's) heart, causing her to add to the Word of Elohim. ("He told me not to <u>touch</u> the tree" – when she'd only heard Him say not to <u>eat</u> of it.) And this would be the beginning of men and women adding to and subtracting from His Word to this very day (see Genesis 3:1-3).

Yes, through adding and subtracting, emphasizing and de-emphasizing, twisting and turning (the Word), leaders and their followers would submit to every wind of doctrine under the sun except the one laid out in the Scriptures. *(Imagine that.)*

They would say things like: "I'm of Calvin, I'm of Luther, I'm of Apollos, I'm of Paul, I'm Baptist, I'm Presbyterian, I'm Church of Christ, I'm Apostolic, I'm Catholic, I'm Methodist, I'm

Let Yahshua Rock Your World

Charismatic, I'm Non-Denominational" and on and on... *I think you get the picture.* Having convinced each group that they are the ones with the truth, I would keep them busy defending their doctrines rather than searching the Scriptures to find out the things that please the Father and His Son.

The delusion and deception would be so strong that they would fall into the trap of defending those "man-made" beliefs, even putting them above the True Word of Elohim. As a result, I'd be able to establish thousands of denominations...each believing its doctrines and creeds were correct. You might call it "Burger King Christianity" – have it **your** way. *(This would be my little inside joke.)*

Of course to legitimize these doctrines, I would have them taught in Theological Seminaries and Christian Universities. Then I would use man's desire to belong to a community of like-minded people to draw them into the different denominations.

Next, I would water down the original language of the Scriptures using a multitude of translations – weaving just enough deception so as not to cause any "red flags" to pop up. Subtle additions and omissions to support my lies, would easily lead the people astray – because the more inaccurate the translation the better chance I'd have of advancing my agenda. No one would think to go back to the original meaning of the words. Truth would then be "**lost in translation**."

I would especially blind them with a false FORM of worship by using a false DEFINITION of sin *(for more about this, see*

If I Were The Enemy

Chapter 5 and Appendix 6). They'd end up with a "form" of Godliness but deny the power therein.

Let's take a closer look at some of the specific ways I would cause people to worship me, *the enemy of Elohim.*

I WOULD:

> ➤ **Cause** them to stop using the <u>true</u> Name of the Father and the Son, thereby keeping them powerless, because there is power in the Set-Apart (Holy) Name. The name they would call upon to be saved would be another name. Since every knee shall bow and every tongue shall confess the Name when it is restored in the end, I would keep everyone blind to it as long as I could. How? I would replace the Name with *titles* and the names of *pagan gods*. Yes, I'd change the Name more than 6,800 times in the Scriptures.

> ➤ **Institute** my festivals (pagan holidays), and cause them to worship me [unknowingly] while thinking that they were worshipping Him. I would hide the origins of my festivals, but if anyone became suspicious I'd just say they have been Christianized and are now an acceptable form of worship to Him. This could be introduced during the 4th century A.D. and by the 21st century the whole world would be celebrating my holidays. Christianity would become nothing more than *paganism* dressed up in new clothes.

> Here are some of the customs from one of my festivals – see if you recognize it.

Let Yahshua Rock Your World

[The Feast of Sol Invictus (Winter Solstice) on December 25th in honor of the sun with Yule logs, mistletoe, ivy, holly wreaths, a tree chopped down with an axe and fastened with nails and hammers and decorated with gold and silver, businesses close and people exchange gifts.]

You might ask how I would make the switch from His Festivals which are *"Divine Appointments"* to my unholy ones. How would I pull it off exactly?

Okay, here's my dirty little secret: The Creator calls **His** Festivals "appointed times" ("Mo'edim" in Hebrew), times that He has ordained from the beginning to meet with His people [His wedding rehearsals if you will]. He even calls them **HIS Festivals**, but I would call then *"Jewish Festivals."* That's how I would blind people to His Truth.

All I'd have to say is that the Biblical Festivals are "only for the Jews," and not for Christians. Believe it or not, my words would immediately override **His Word** in the minds of the people. *(Of course I would hide the fact that all Israel is not Jewish…that Judah is only (1) one of the twelve tribes of Israel. There are other tribes scattered all over the world who for the most part don't even know who they are.)*

To cement the idea of His Festivals being Jewish in the minds of the people, I would say, *"It's in the Old Covenant and you don't have to do that anymore. You're no longer under the Law; you're under grace."* Now you'll have to admit that one would work like a charm.

If I Were The Enemy

Starting these lies around the second century would give me enough time to thoroughly deceive the whole world before His return. Just call me the "Master Deceiver – *the father of lies.*"

Using statements like, "it's for the Jews" or "it's in the Old Covenant" to answer any resistance, I would have the entire arsenal needed to deceive even the very elect. It wouldn't even matter that the Messiah as well as His disciples kept **His** Festivals. And it wouldn't matter that all the first century believers kept them for some thirty years after the Messiah's death. *(None of that would matter.)* All I'd have to say is: "That's Jewish!"

(**Don't believe me?** *Just take a survey at your Church next Sunday. Ask as many people as you can if they have ever celebrated* Pesach *(Passover),* Hag HaMatsch *(Unleavened Bread),* Bikkurim *(First Fruits),* Shavuot *(Pentecost),* Yom Teruah *(Feast of Trumpets),* Yom Kippur *(Day of Atonement), or* Succoth *(Feast of Tabernacles). Even in the so called Mega-churches, with thousands in attendance, it's doubtful that you will find more than a handful. Then ask who celebrates Christmas, Easter, Halloween, or Valentine's Day, and you'll likely get a positive response from just about everyone.* **The end result is: The latter won't have any oil in their lamps and they won't be watching for His return because "oil" and "His return" are both tied to** His **Festivals**.)

Let Yahshua Rock Your World

- **Change** the day that the Creator has made Holy (Set-Apart) for man to worship Him. I would change it to any other day than *"that day,"* but preferably to the day on which I would have been worshipped by pagans for centuries – Sun-god day. Most would never know the difference.

  All I would have to do in order to deceive them into thinking the day had been changed from the Sabbath (seventh day) to Sunday (first day), is to convince them that Messiah died on Friday and rose on Sunday; (never mind that there's NOT ONE VERSE in the entire Scriptures that mentions it was changed – and what really makes me laugh with evil delight is you can't even get 3 days and 3 nights counting from Friday to Sunday).

  If anyone started to get suspicious, I'd just tell them that it's referring to three partial days, and that should do it. His example of Jonah being in the belly of the fish for **three days** and **three nights** would be nullified. And, since they would be blinded to the true Feast Days (HIS FESTIVALS), they wouldn't pick up on the fact that the Sabbath spoken of in John 19:31 was a High Feast Day and not the regular weekly Sabbath on Saturday. *Am I deceptive or what? (For more on this, see Chapter 4.)*

- **Trick** them into thinking they are no longer "under the Law," but "under grace." Oh, this would be one of my all time favorites. As a dear friend of mine would say, "Them is fighting words right there boy." Nothing else would get

If I Were The Enemy

spiritual feathers ruffled as much as the notion of: "to be or not to be *under the Law*." This message would be preached with extreme conviction from pulpits across the land causing visions of *shackles and bondage* in congregations everywhere. To convince any skeptics, I would back it up with enough Scripture (taken out of context of course and mistranslated) to deceive those who are not rightly dividing the Word. *Good plan don't you think? I'm so clever.*

Ironically, people will obey the laws of the land – even though there are thousands of them. They'll say, "I'm a law-abiding citizen." But when I get through twisting the Scriptures, they will be easily swayed NOT to obey Elohim's Law, which by the way brings blessings beyond measure. *Shhh!* I'll just keep them focused on obeying man's laws ONLY – not running a red light, or driving without a license or car insurance. "Buckle up for safety" and "click it or ticket" will become familiar slogans.

Another tactic that I'd use is the man-made doctrine of "dispensationalism." I'd dispense a little "sationalism" here and a little "sationalism" there until I'd be able to convince multiple thousands that the "Church" has replaced Israel; that the New Covenant is for Christians and the Old Covenant is for the Jews. *(Many would believe.)* I would even convince publishers to put a blank page in the Bible to separate the "Old Covenant" from the "New Covenant" to reinforce my lie.

Consequently, when people read about Israel in their daily newspapers, they would not understand that Bible prophecy was being fulfilled right before their very eyes. Because of "Replacement Theology," many would not believe the Land of Israel is important to Elohim, even though He said the Land of Israel is His land; He even placed His Name in Jerusalem and He can give the Land to whomever He pleases. *(Sadly for America, whatever nation participates in dividing His land will be judged Zechariah 12:3, 9).*

Without understanding that Israel is the "Apple" of His eye, they would never put 2 and 2 together and make the connection that every time America pressures Israel into giving up land something really bad happens in America. It will even be documented by a Washington Press Core Correspondent that Hurricane Katrina was one such event, but most would never see that parallel.

Therefore, Bible prophecy would go right over their heads as it was unfolding before their eyes. I would keep them focused on the ECONOMY and on propagating their false doctrines – leading the un-learned astray.

Back to dispensationalism: John Darby is the person I would chose to introduce the doctrine of dispensationalism in the 1800's. Darby's doctrine would later be made popular in the United States by Cyrus Scofield's Scofield Reference Bible. Darby's beliefs would be spread so effectively that they would still be taught in various forms even as late as the

If I Were The Enemy

year 2009 in Theological Seminaries and Christian Universities and by popular Christian authors.

And since the end is prophesied out of the beginning, according to Isaiah 46:8-10, my separation of the Old Covenant from the New Covenant would make it possible for me to hide while I operate my deception right in the midst of His people. Making them believe that the Savior only shows up in the New Covenant and that He came to free the Church from the Law, gives me great pleasure. And when the church leaders buy into this lie (hook, line and sinker), A REALLY BIG ROCK of "Titanic" proportions lies ahead!

Adding insult to injury, I would then deceive the leaders into misinterpreting Paul's letters, *(from a Western, Greco-Roman mindset of course)* and they would spread my lie far and wide – leading many sheep astray.

Again, we're no longer under the "Law" but under "grace" would be the mantra of leaders in the Church. And because of my success in convincing the Church that it's under the New Covenant, I'd be able to keep it a secret that **there's more "grace" in the Old Covenant than in the New and there is more "Law" in the New Covenant than in the Old.** *WOW when I'm evil I'm evil!*

Keeping His people out of the Old Covenant would certainly keep them far away from Psalm 119 where it's written that His Law is: eternal, everlasting, righteous, endures forever, a blessing, a delight, life-giving, strength, truth, trustworthy, comforting, gracious, better than gold and silver, sure, makes one wiser, gives more understanding, sweeter than honey, a lamp to my feet, a light to my path, my heritage, the joy of my heart, my hiding place, my shield, my hope, wonderful, light, true, founded forever, awesome, and peace-giving.

(If anyone ever stumbled upon this Psalm, I'd just plant in their minds that it's too long to read and encourage them to move on to some other reading. If that didn't work I would revert to "It's in the Old Covenant and doesn't apply today.")

Spiritual anarchy would become the norm. The "Church" would look just like the world – without any distinguishing marks. Paul's teachings would be as clear as mud. And Elohim's "LAW" would become a "ROCK of offense."

(Oops. Watch out for that Millstone!)

- **Change** the calendar, established by Elohim, to a man-made calendar using the names of pagan gods for months of the year and days of the week. With this calendar I would throw them off track as to how close they are to the end of His 6th / $6,000^{th}$ day / year. There would be no watching or waiting, just marrying and giving in marriage like in the days of Noah. And without any understanding of the Biblical (not Jewish) Feasts they would never figure out the season of His return.

- **Convince** them that they are free to eat anything they want to eat – clean or unclean. "Bring on the pork baby especially that Easter Ham." All I'd have to do is take a few scriptures out of context, veil the cultural setting and add some words that don't even appear in the original texts to make the Messiah appear to say something that He didn't say at all like (…MAKING ALL FOODS CLEAN).

> **Keep** those translations coming, the more inaccurate they are, the better for me to hide the truth. I would even publish a new one that's really easy to understand in today's language that would not use evening and morning for the reckoning of days, distorting when a Biblical day begins and ends. I would create havoc with that version.

> **Make** His people miss the blessing of obedience to His Ways (the Torah / Law / Instructions) so that they won't have oil in their lamps – just like the five foolish virgins who missed the wedding. He will have to say to them, "Depart from Me, I never **knew** you."

Now you know my secrets – how I would kill, steal and destroy His people by making them *think* they were worshipping Him in Spirit and in Truth when they were not. To my delight on *that day* many would say, "…**'Master, Master, have we not prophesied in Your Name, and cast out demons in Your Name, and done many mighty works in Your Name?' And then I shall declare to them, 'I never knew you, depart from Me, you who work lawlessness!'** " According to 1 John 3:4, sin is lawlessness and the Law (Instructions) is the Torah so sin is **Torahlessness**.

Let Yahshua Rock Your World

I must confess that there is one thing that would disturb me and that is the fulfillment of prophecy. It has been prophesied that the spirit of Elijah will come and restore ALL things in the end: His Name, His Language, His Festivals (appointed times), His weekly Sabbaths, His Commandments (ALL TEN), and His Dietary Laws. And He has already started calling out His remnant – their numbers are growing rapidly. So all I can do is work as fast as I can to deceive as many as I can for as long as I can.

Let's dig deep – down to the bed-ROCK – and get to the bottom of His foundation!

"...They made their faces harder than rock,
they refused to turn back."
(Jeremiah 5:3)

Chapter 2: Idioms

ENGLISH IDIOMS

Idiom is defined in Webster's New World Dictionary as: **1)** the language or dialect of a people, region, class, etc., **2)** the usual way that the words of a language are joined to express thought, **3)** a phrase or expression with an unusual syntactic pattern or with a meaning differing from the literal meaning of its parts.

From the above definition, it's easy to understand how important it is not only to learn a language but the *culture as well*. Learning the culture will greatly increase our ability to comprehend what is being communicated.

I was amazed at how mistaken I'd been about many verses of Scripture because I did not recognize the idioms.

For example, just imagine for a moment, that you live in a foreign country and you do not know anything about America, but you've decided to take a trip to America to find out everything you can about the people and their customs. When you return to your country, you might report something like this:

Their bodies are incredible. They can "play music by ear," and sometimes they are "all ears." It's easy for them to "lend an ear" to someone or "keep an ear to the ground." They have "eyes in the back of their head," and when they "keep their eyes peeled," they have "eyes like a hawk." Sometimes their "blood boils," other times it "runs cold." Some even have "green thumbs." And occasionally, they get "frogs in their throats." They can either "wear their hearts on their sleeves" or "eat their hearts out."

Their legal system is different. Some Lawyers are "ambulance chasers" and they will "take you for a ride" or "take you to the cleaners."

How performers become successful. They "break a leg" and "knock 'em dead."

What are their children like? Some are "a chip off the old block." But if they don't "cut the mustard," they are called the "black sheep of the family."

What is it like to shop there? Sometimes they're willing to "give their right arm" for something. At other times, they'll "give an arm and a leg." And in small towns the "sidewalks roll up" at 6:00 p.m.

From the previous illustrations, can you see how difficult it would be for a person from another country (who knew nothing about America) to comprehend what's being communicated if that person didn't understand the cultural idioms in our language? In 2

Idioms

Timothy 2:15 we are instructed to study to show ourselves approved to Elohim, a worker who has no need to be ashamed, rightly handling the word of truth.

To rightly handle the word of truth, we have to be able to recognize Hebraic idioms (cultural phrases) when we see them. Once we become familiar with what they are and how they are used in the Scriptures, meanings become crystal clear. Otherwise, misinterpretation will be the predicted outcome.

Also, when we have an opportunity to get back to the original meaning of words before they are watered down through several languages and numerous translations, we can take a *giant step* forward towards understanding what our Creator is communicating to us.

Just consider the way meanings of words have changed over time. When I was young, the word "gay" meant something totally different than it does today. And now "mouse" has two meanings – no longer is it just a small four legged animal with a long tail – it is also a device used with computers.

The unique feature of the Hebrew language that makes it different from any other language is that it is concrete rather than abstract – its meaning does not change over time. That's why it's considered a pure language. And it is the one that's being restored in these last days. Unfortunately, Western seminaries offer a higher ratio of Greek courses to Hebrew courses – 9 to 1 is not unusual.

Okay, here's my last English idiom. I "double dog dare you" to keep reading.

HEBRAIC IDIOMS

Again, there are many Hebraic idioms in the Old and New Covenant and if we don't know what they mean, we won't have a clue about what's being communicated. Our belief system can be altered if an idiom is translated literally and we don't know the cultural meaning behind it. This has led to much confusion in the Church. It can be quite shocking to find out that what you think you know isn't so.

Hebrew is an amazing language. Each Hebrew letter is full of meaning and symbolism. In English an "a" is an "a" and nothing more. However in Hebrew, each letter is a word. It has an assigned number, and has a word picture based upon ancient scripts. The first letter of the Paleo Hebrew language for example is an Alef (𐤀) which is the picture of an Ox – signifying "strength" in addition to "leader," the "first," the "beginning." It has a numeric value of one.

The Hebrew mindset is always more interested in function than appearance. For instance, if you ask someone with a Hebraic understanding to describe a pencil he will say, "You write with it," while someone with a Greek / Western mindset will likely describe it as about 6 inches long, shaped like a straw, about $5/16^{th}$ inch in diameter, with lead in the center.

Therefore, when we start to look at the Scriptures from a "Hebraic Perspective," we are looking at the original intent that the Father already clearly defined in the Tanakh (Old Covenant) that has virtually been ignored by Western Christians. However,

Idioms

without knowing how the B'rit Hadashah (New Covenant) writers looked at life and the various idioms and peculiar phrases, it would be impossible to interpret everything they spoke about.

Most of what Messiah said meant something totally different in the ears of the New Covenant writers than it does to our ears. For hundreds of years, Hebrew idioms have been translated into English *literally*. When the translators and scholars transform an ancient document by substituting English words for the original Hebrew words, even if the words are translated correctly (and many times they aren't), the original Hebrew thought is lost. The words are there, but the meaning is missing – it is literally lost in the translation!

For example, when Elohim created the sun, moon and stars and said let them be for signs and seasons He was not talking about the seasons of summer, winter, spring, and fall. The Hebrew word used here for seasons is mo'edim, *which means Festivals, Appointed Times.*

Here are some more examples of things that have been lost in translation:

> What is meant by the Hebrew idiom "**Evil Eye**," "**Good Eye**" and "**Bad Eye**" in the Scriptures?

Look at these two versions (the King James Version and the English Standard Version):

> "The light of the body is the eye: if therefore thine **eye be single**, thy whole body shall be full of light. But if thine **eye be evil**, thy whole body shall be full

of darkness…" Matthew 6:22-23, KJV. The ESV reads differently however.

"The eye is the lamp of the body. So if your **eye is healthy**, your whole body will be full of light, but if your **eye is bad**, your whole body will be full of darkness…" (ESV).

In verse twenty-two we go from a *single eye* in the KJV to a *healthy eye* in the ESV and in verse twenty-three in the KJV it shows an *evil eye* whereas the ESV shows a *bad eye*. Other versions express: eye be whole, eye be simple, eye be sound, eye be plain, and eye be sincere, clear, honest, or good.

It appears that the translators had a problem translating this idiom, while the next verse explains it. "No one is able to serve two masters, for either he shall hate the one and love the other, or else he shall cleave to the one and despise the other. You are not able to serve Elohim and mammon" (Matthew 6:24). See also Deuteronomy 15:9-10 and Proverbs 28:22, 27.

You will find that in every instance when Messiah spoke about the eye being "good" or "evil" or "plucking out the eye," He was addressing the issue of GREED. A greedy person was considered to have an evil eye, i.e., a person absorbed with obtaining things for self.

It makes me wonder what Messiah would say about the materialistic "prosperity message" that is pervasive in so many of our churches today where being blessed is equated with how much

Idioms

stuff you have. I have even heard T.V. preachers tell members of their congregation to "fake it until you make it."

That statement flies in the face of what Messiah spoke in Matthew 6:25-34, where He exhorts those with Him to be anxious for nothing – what you will eat or drink – what you will wear. Then He tells them that their faith is *little* if they seek after these things rather than seeking FIRST the Kingdom of Elohim and His righteousness and all these things will be added to you.

Let's get back to the "good eye" Hebrew idiom. Proverbs 22:9 explains the concept of the good eye further. "He who has a good eye is blessed, For he gives of his bread to the poor."

When Messiah talked about plucking out your eye if it causes you to sin in Matthew 18:9, He didn't mean it literally, because that would have been in violation of the Torah in Deuteronomy 14:1 where we're told not to cut ourselves. He was instructing us to run away from greed and idolatry and guard our hearts from the evil eye of want and desire.

Let's dig a little deeper and look at another Hebraic idiom, **"Destroy the Law."**

Matthew 5:17-18 reads, "Think not that I (Yahshua) am come to weaken, or destroy the Torah (Law), or the Neviim (Prophets): I have not come to weaken, or destroy, but to completely reveal it in its intended fullness. For truly I say to you, Until the current shamayim (heavens) and earth pass away, not one yud (jot), or one nekudah (tittle) shall by any means pass from the Torah (Law), until all be fulfilled" (Restoration Scriptures True Name Edition Version).

Messiah said he did not come to destroy the Law and He added that until heaven and earth pass, not one jot or one tittle shall pass from the Law, till ALL be fulfilled. Now the last time I checked, the heaven and the earth have not passed away. So why is it that you can walk into almost any Church on Sunday morning and hear from the pulpit that the Law has been done away with – Jesus fulfilled it when He said, "It is finished?"

"Destroy the Law" and **"Fulfill the Law"** are Hebrew idioms. "Destroy" and "fulfill" are technical terms used by the rabbis when they argued points of the Law. According to Bivin and Blizzard in their book *Understanding the Difficult Words of Jesus,* when a sage felt that a colleague had misinterpreted a passage of Scripture, he would say, "You are destroying the Law!" Needless to say, in most cases, his colleagues strongly disagreed. What was "destroying the Law" for one sage was "fulfilling the Law" (correctly interpreting Scripture) for another.

When you read the New Covenant with that understanding in mind you will see that a great deal of Messiah's ministry was spent giving a correct interpretation of the Law – not doing away with the Law. He actually kept the Law. As a matter of fact if you want to get technical about it – He is the Law. ***He came to fill it up with meaning***.

As an example, you may recall that He healed people on the Sabbath and the Pharisees went ballistic. Then He taught that it was the right (righteous) thing to do on the Sabbath. But He never did away with the Sabbath. He was showing them the Spirit of the

Idioms

Law and that their legalistic observance was wrong (unrighteous). We'll cover more about that later in chapter 5, "It's The Law."

(By the way, have you ever wondered what a jot and tittle are? A jot is the smallest letter in the Hebrew alphabet, "yod (׳). " A tittle is the decorative spur [merest ornament] on a Hebrew letter.)

What is a "Prayer Closet"?

I can remember sitting in Church and being told to go home and get alone with God in my "prayer closet," to pray. Little did I know that this was an idiom and that it was not literally talking about a physical closet, but was something entirely different. Don't get me wrong, there is nothing wrong with praying in a closet if that's what you want to do, but that is not what the Scripture is referring to.

The first century Israelites carried their "prayer closet" with them wherever they went.

A "prayer closet" is a tah-lit (tah-leet), which is Hebrew for "tent-little," translated in English, "little tent." The tah-lit is often referred to in English as a "prayer shawl" or "prayer closet."

The "prayer closet" is worn over the shoulders and during prayer it is pulled toward the face by both hands to signify "closing the door of your closet." This was done because the millions of Israelites who would gather at the Tent of Meeting could not all fit inside. So, they would wear their own "little tent" and pray as a way of joining their brothers and sisters who were in the Tent of Meeting.

Those who went "into their prayer closets" were praying alongside everyone else at the Tent of Meeting, whether inside the tent or outside the tent by going into their little tents. Knowing what a prayer closet is can also give us some idea of the likelihood that Paul may very well have been a "little tent" or "prayer closet" maker.

"Let the Dead Bury the Dead"

I stumbled over this one for a long time because it sounded so harsh. However, it's a Hebrew idiom that has been shredded by Western theological thought. When Messiah said to a "would-be" disciple who wanted to bury his father first, "Let the dead bury the dead," what was He really saying? This statement is in reference to the "second-burial" system of that time, when the Hellenized Jews were influenced by Gnosticism. These Jews would bury their loved one and one year later dig up the body and place the bones in an ossuary (bone box). They believed that the one year between burials was a time of redemption when the "sinful" flesh was removed, thereby doing away with the sin so that the body could now be buried sinless with its ancestors.

Messiah's words to this "would-be" disciple were actually to say, "Hog-wash! Your father has been dead for a year. Let's go!"

"Eternal Life"

Inheriting eternal life is a Hebrew idiom for "living life in the will of God." This meant that those who followed the Messiah believed that if they obeyed His teachings and imitated His ways of living out Elohim's will, they would gain the ability to "live their lives in the will of Elohim" (inherit eternal life) because they believed that

Idioms

Messiah's interpretations of the commands of the Father in the Torah were the perfect interpretations.

"Healing in His Wings"

This is "the hem of His garment" which is referring to the tzitzi (fringes / tassels) on His tallit (prayer shawl).

A Hebrew concept that is often missed in English translations concerns the woman with the issue of blood in Matthew 9:21, who said within herself, "If I only touch His garment, I shall be healed." Verse 20 shows that it was the hem of His garment that she desired to touch. In the Hebrew, the term "hem" is the same as the word "fringes" or "wing," and is a common word for the border of the prayer shawl worn by Messiah and the Yahudi (Jewish) men of the first century. This fringe is called the tzitzit (pronounced zeet zeet) that was worn on any four cornered garment in accordance with the commandment of Numbers 15:38-41, to remind them of the Father's Commandments.

> "Speak to the children of Yisra'ĕl (Israel), and you shall say to them to make tzitziyot (plural for tzitzit-- tassel) on the corners of their garments throughout their generations, and to put a blue cord in the tzitzit (tassel) of the corners. And it shall be to you for a tzitzit, and you shall see it, and shall remember all the commands of Yahweh and shall do them, and not search after your own heart and your own eyes after which you went whoring…" (Numbers 15: 38-39).

During Messiah's day the men dressed primarily in a halluq (ha-luke), which was a simple tunic worn both at home and at work. The halluq is usually made of linen and covers the body all the way to the middle of the shin. When appearing in public, the men covered their halluq with a large rectangular cloth that draped over the shoulder and fell to the ankles. This cloth was called a tallit (ta-leet), and served as protection from the cold or rain. Hanging from the end of each of its four corners was a tzitzit in obedience to the Biblical command. Today, the tallit has become the term used for the prayer shawl.

During the first century, there was an understanding concerning Messiah that was associated with the tzitzit. It was prophesied in Malachi 4:2 that when the Messiah came He would have "healing in His wings." Remember, in Hebrew the term for hem, fringe, or border is the same as wings. When someone pulled the prayer shawl over the head in prayer, it appeared as if he had wings. Psalm 91:1-4 is referring to the prayer shawl as well when it describes dwelling in the secret places of the Most High and being under His wings.

When one realizes the significance of this text in the Hebraic concept, it becomes clear why the woman in Luke 8:44 was healed. By faith, she was expressing her belief in Messiah as the Son of Righteousness with healing in His wings, and declaring Elohim's Word was true.

"Sun of Righteousness"
A Hebrew figure-of-speech or idiom, which means "the Messiah."

"Bind" and "Loose"

This is another Hebrew idiom; "bind" meaning "prohibit" and "loose" meaning "permit" (Matthew 16:19; 18:18).

In Hebraic understanding, it is an accepted legal designation. In Matthew 16:19 where Messiah gives Peter the keys to the Kingdom and says, "...whatever you bind on earth shall be having been bound in the heavens, and whatever you loosen on earth shall be having been loosened in the heavens," is often misunderstood and has caused enormous confusion. This phrase meant that what we allow on earth should be what is allowed in the heavens. And what we prohibit on earth should be what is prohibited in the heavens.

Not understanding this Hebraic idiom has resulted in Christians binding and loosing the devil and everything else under the sun that you can think of.

Messiah's deliverance ministry was not about binding and loosing every unclean spirit in the world – He could have done that – but He didn't. He could have given out stronghold surveys and told people to wait until a group of trained deliverance ministers were ready, but He didn't.

The first century rabbis were constantly called upon by their community to interpret scriptural commands. For example, the Scriptures forbid working on the Sabbath, but do not define what constitutes work. As a result, the rabbis were required to rule on which activities were permitted on the Sabbath. In other words, they determined what things were already **bound** in Heaven and what things were already **loosed** in Heaven.

Let Yahshua Rock Your World

Food for thought: "There are over 5,366 manuscripts of the New Covenant in Greek, each differing from the other and containing several hundred variants. However, in each one of these manuscripts there are idioms which are almost meaningless in any language—including Greek—except in Hebrew! How can such a thing be explained unless it is because the original was Hebrew? There are many of these Hebraisms, one of the most common of them being '**Son of man**.' What does 'Son of man' mean in English, Spanish, German, in any language? Absolutely nothing—except for Hebrew. The expression 'Ben Adam' means literally 'son of Adam' and by extension 'son of man,' and 'man,' Adam being of course the first man alive. In any street corner in Israel you may hear 'here comes this Ben Adam,' meaning 'here comes this man.' This example, which occurs no less than 92 times in the Tanakh (the Old Covenant) and 43 times in the New Covenant according to Cruden's Concordance is obviously the same Hebrew Idiom.

"Let us take another example, the idiom 'Peace be to you,' appearing twelve times in the New Covenant. What kind of a greeting is '**Peace be to you**' in English, Spanish, French, or any other language—except in Hebrew? It is meaningless, again. Only in Hebrew does it make any real sense. This is the most common, everyday greeting in Israel today, the worldwide famous 'shalom,' literally 'peace,' but really an everyday greeting meaning anything from 'Hi,' to 'How are you?' according to the intonation and the mood of the speaker." (Bivin and Blizzard Jr., op cit pp. 55-56, 59-60)

From the short list in this chapter, can you see how important it is to study the Hebrew roots of our faith to gain a better

Idioms

understanding of Elohim's Word? Would you agree there is at least a possibility that we have missed some key elements to understanding the Scriptures because we haven't understood the culture or the language in which it was written? *(See Appendix 1 for more Hebrew idioms)*

The Hebrew language is truly amazing. There is even a prophecy in the exact order of the Hebrew Alphabet.

Alef (א) = Ox (Strength, leader, the first, the beginning), *Colossians 1:13-16* "…the first-born of all creation…"

Beth (ב) = House, *1 Samuel 2:35* "…And I shall build him a steadfast house…"

Gimel (ג) = Camel – benefits (to be loaded with benefits), *Psalm 103:2* "…And do not forget all His dealings…"

Daleth (ד) = Door – the way, *Psalm 119:30* "…I have chosen the way of truth…"

Hay (ה) = Window – to behold, to reveal, *Ezekiel 44:4* "…I looked and saw the esteem of Yahweh…"

Waw (ו) = hook, nail (it means it attaches things like a conjunction – we need to be attached to His Word), *Psalm 119:44-45* "…That I might guard Your Torah (Law) continually, Forever and ever…"

Let Yahshua Rock Your World

Zayin (ז) = Weapon, *Isaiah 54:17* "No weapon formed against you shall prosper…"

Heth (ח) = Fence or a hedge (He made a heth or hedge around Job), *Job 3:23* "…whom Eloah has hedged in?"

Teth (ט) = Winding, surround, *Psalm 125:2* "As the mountains surround Yerushalayim (Jerusalem), So Yahweh surrounds His people, Now and forever."

Yod (י) = Hand (Your Hands-Yodim), *Psalm 119:73* "Your hands have made me…"

Kaph (כ) = Bent hand, palm, open hand, *Isaiah 49:16* "See, I have inscribed you on the palms of My hands…"

Lamed (ל) = Good shepherd's staff (authority / teachers / rulership comes with Lamed), *John 10:14* "I am the Good Shepherd. And I know Mine, and Mine know Me…"

Mem (מ) = Water, sea (land = Israel, sea = nations), *Revelation 22:1-3* "And he showed me a river of water of life…"

Nun (נ) = Fish, life, *Genesis 1:28* "…and rule over the fish of the sea…"

Samek (ס) = Prop up / support, *John 12:32* "…I am lifted up from the earth…"

Idioms

Ayin (ע) = Eye, to see, *Revelation 1:7* "...and every eye shall see Him..."

Pe (פ) = Mouth, *Romans 3:19* "...so that every mouth might be stopped..."

Tzadee (צ) = Hook, fish hook, *John 12:32* "...shall draw all *men* unto Myself."

Koph (ק) = Needle-eye, back of the head (the least), the back, *Hebrews 8:11* "...they all shall know Me, from the least of them to the greatest of them."

Resh (ר) = Head, head of the year (Rosh), *Exodus 12:2* "This month is the beginning of months for you, it is the first month of the year for you."

Shin (ש) = Tooth, teeth, to consume, *Genesis 49:12* "...and His teeth whiter than milk."

Tau (ת) = Mark (x) sign, *Ezekiel 9:4-6* "...put a mark on the foreheads of the men..."

Yahshua (Jesus) was the **b**eginning and the source of creation. He built a **h**ouse for our **b**enefit. Elohim opened the **d**oor and made the way into His Kingdom that we may **b**ehold His glory in the house by **a**ttaching ourselves to His Torah. No **w**eapon formed against us will prosper for He is our **h**edge of protection **s**urrounding us with His presence. His **h**ands have made us. He engraved us on the **p**alm of His hands. By keeping His Covenants and teachings, we have **a**uthority to rule over His **s**ea of nations and all **l**ife therein. When He is **l**ifted up for all who pierced Him to **s**ee, every **m**outh will be stopped as He **d**raws all humanity to Himself from the **l**east to the **g**reatest for as a **c**onsuming fire He will destroy the wicked and deliver those He has **m**arked with His sign. (Biltz, Mark. Audio Torah Parsha. 2007. www.elshaddaiministries.us)

INCREDIBLE!

"YAHWEH [the LORD] lives! And blessed is my Rock! And exalted is my Elohim, The Rock of my deliverance…"
(2 Samuel 22:47)

Chapter 3:
What's In A Name?

"A *good* name is better than precious oil..."
(Ecclesiastes 7:1)

"A *good* name is preferable to great riches."
(Proverbs 22:1)

A year ago, at a close friend's surprise birthday party, I became aware of a desire that seems to be embedded in the hearts of men.

We were anxiously awaiting Kim's arrival and many of us had not seen each other in several months – and for some it had been years. So this party served not only to honor our friend's birthday, but it was another intersection in the lives of those who had not seen each other for a long time.

There were many "catch up" conversations mixed with the anticipation of his arrival. With cell phone in hand, the "Activity Coordinator" (his daughter) quietly monitored his every move toward the party destination.

Let Yahshua Rock Your World

The band was on standby and food was spread and waiting as we received constant updates on the proximity of the vehicle carrying Kim and his wife. As you can imagine, everyone was elated when the call came that Kim had finally arrived. Happy birthday yells, smiles, hand-clapping, and live music greeted him. It became apparent very quickly that he was surprised beyond a shadow of a doubt – he didn't have a clue; he *was* SURPRISED!

What a delightful party for a wonderful friend. Eventually, the Activity Coordinator instructed everyone who wanted to participate to come forward and share their thoughts about Kim. One-by-one friends and family reminisced over the microphone in "roast-like" statements about their relationship with Kim through the years. *(This was a real heartfelt moment.)* These funny stories painted pictures that made you laugh, shake your head in agreement, and grab your stomach all at the same time. Finally, it was time for Kim to "make a speech." He talked about the desires of his heart.

He said the thing he desired most in this life was to have his family NAME continue. That's when it hit me…

I knew from reading the Scriptures how important and valuable our Heavenly Father's Name and His Son's Name are. After all, salvation is in His Name; demons tremble at His Name; every knee shall bow in His Name; His Name is above every other name that is named in heaven and in the earth. His disciples turned the known world upside down using His Name.

So, why is it that so few believers know His true Name? It has been hidden for centuries, but is now being restored in these last days.

What's In A Name?

You may be as amazed as I was when I discovered that the Creator's Name has been replaced 6,823 times. That's right, in nearly all translations our Creator's Hebrew Name has been replaced *6,823 times*? For His Name to appear that many times in the original Scriptures, I believe He wants us to know His Name and use His Name. On the contrary, for it to have been replaced that many times with a title or some pagan name, I believe someone else does **not** want us to know and use it. What do you believe?

When I found out that the letter "J" was not in any language until the 16th century, it was a "Kodak" moment for me. Even today the letter "J" does not exist in the Hebrew, Aramaic or Greek alphabet. It's actually less than 500 years old. So, contrary to popular belief, our Savior's Name is not Jesus. Shocking? It certainly was for me. The name "Jesus" has only been in existence since the year 1559 A.D.

When I learned these truths, it was one of those jaw-dropping, wide-eyed, eyebrow-raising, take-your-breath-away events. Having heard the name "Jesus" all my life, this was a hard "ROCK-pill" to swallow at first, but after doing some research on my own, I realized that the Savior NEVER heard anyone *(including His mother)* call him Jesus.

Now if my name was Betty and let's say you were my friend, but you called me Sally every time you spoke to me I wouldn't think you were a close friend. And if your name was Sam but I called you Michael every time I saw you, would you love to hear the wrong name? But then let's say one day I got it right and called you by your real name, Sam, how would that make you feel?

During the course of your life you have probably heard men express the same desire that my dear friend expressed at his surprise birthday party – "…that my family NAME continues." You see, names mean things; it represents your character, and perhaps your family's standing in the community, etc. You may have heard a parent say something like this to their child: "You are a Franklin and the Franklins' don't act like that."

There are a lot of man-made traditions in Judaism *AND* there are a lot of man-made traditions in Christianity as well. False doctrines that were perpetrated before any of us were even born have caused the Name above all names to be replaced and put into non-use, thereby making millions (unknowingly) break the **Third Commandment**. *It's a tragedy.*

If there's no distinction between His Name and that of the pagans, you could have a worship service where Christians, Muslims, Satan Worshippers, Hindus, and Buddhist were all singing songs with these words: "The Lord reigns. He is a mighty God, the Lord God reigns"; "Great is the Lord"; "Our God is an Awesome God"; or "I am a friend of God." This would not be a problem for any of these groups because they all have gods and lords.

You may be thinking – the case (upper or lower) of the letters makes all the difference. Well, that's what I thought too, but I found out that in the Hebrew language there are no upper and lower case letters. So there goes that defense.

What's In A Name?

(Let's get back to the worship service.)

All these groups would appear to be in unity, but in truth they are not worshipping the same deity. You could say to a Muslim, "I love God" and the Muslim could say "I love God too, and his name is Allah." And believe it or not some Christians believe that Allah is the same as the Elohim (God) of Abraham, Isaac and Jacob, because they haven't been taught His true Name. This is another example of how the enemy is attempting to destroy us. Hosea 4:6 declares, "My people have perished for lack of knowledge…"

It's true that He looks on the heart, but in these last days He is restoring His Name as He prophesied in the Scriptures. How wonderful it is to exalt and esteem and meditate on His true Name.

We are told His Name is Holy and when we repeat the prayer in Matthew 6:9 (KJV) we say, "…Hallowed be thy name." The Hebrew word for Hallowed is Kadosh which means Set-Apart (Holy). If we call Him generic titles like God, Lord, Christ, Jehovah or HaShem, etc. we are not setting His Name apart; we are not Hallowing His Name.

In Proverbs 30:4 we see that He wants us to know His Name as well as His power:

> "Who has gone up to the heavens and come down? Who has gathered the wind in His fists? Who has bound the waters in a garment? Who established all the ends of the earth? **What is His Name, And what is His Son's Name, If you know it?"**

Let Yahshua Rock Your World

Most Christians can't answer that question because they don't know the Name of their Elohim. His name is YHWH. The letters are pronounced Yud Hay Waw Hay and His name is usually pronounced Yahweh (Yah-way). Isaiah 42:8 says, "I am Yahweh that is My Name, and My esteem I do not give to another, nor My praise to idols." His Name means I AM WHO I AM – Yahweh that Always Was, that Always Is, and That Ever Is to Come. His Name represents HIS POWER and HIS AUTHORITY!

In the ancient Paleo Hebrew picture language, **Yud** (𐤉) is the picture of a hand, **Hay** (𐤄) is the picture of a window (meant to reveal), and **Waw** (𐤅) is a picture of a nail (to connect or hold things together). Yahweh's name pictographically is the hand revealed the nail revealed. His Son's Name is Yahshua which means YHWH (Yahweh) is salvation. So when Thomas saw His nail scared hands he said, "My Yahweh and my Elohim." The Father and the Son both have Hebrew names that are full of meaning.

At first it was awkward for my brain to convert the titles "God" and "Lord" to His Hebrew Name, and I had difficulty replacing the name Jesus with Yahshua as well. But with practice, it started to flow more naturally. Do I still say God and Lord? Occasionally (because of so many years of indoctrination), but my desire is to please Him by practicing the use of His Name. You can do it too – if you so desire.

Once you've done your research and you have the revelation that He does have a personal Name and you decide to start using it, you will have to overcome resistance on two fronts. First, since we've all been brainwashed in the *"non-use"* of it, you are likely to stumble for

What's In A Name?

a while but I encourage you to keep practicing and before you know it the words "God," "Lord," "HaShem," etc., will no longer pop out of your mouth automatically. *(The use of titles for His Name will become less and less.)* In no way am I trying to be dogmatic or legalistic about it – it's just one of the ways I try to please Him.

The second front you'll have to overcome when you make the decision to use His Name is the response from those who have not been informed. This is a great opportunity for you to witness to them *in love*. We should never use any revelation or knowledge the Father gives us to beat someone up with it. And don't get mad at your pastor or anyone else in your Church for not teaching these things. They can only teach what they've been taught and remember the deception has been passed down for centuries.

Yirmeyahu (Jeremiah) prophesied that Elohim would make us know once and for all His Name, His power and His might. Jeremiah 16:21 says, **"they shall know that My Name is Yahweh."** Your translation probably reads, "…and they shall know that my name is The Lord." How sad. It's just one of more than 6,000 places where the English translators changed His Name to a title. The original text shows His Hebrew Name.

If this is the first time you've heard about His true Name, it's not your fault. The generic names and titles have been around for centuries. According to Yirmeyahu (Jeremiah) we have inherited lies:

> "O Yahweh, my strength and my stronghold and
> my refuge, in the day of distress the gentiles shall
> come to You from the ends of the earth and say,

Let Yahshua Rock Your World

Our fathers have inherited only falsehood, futility, and there is no value in them. Would a man make mighty ones for himself, which are not mighty ones" (Jeremiah 16:19-20)?

In ONE instance, the translators left His true Name in tact in Psalms 68:4, where it reads, "Sing to Elohim, sing praises to His Name. Raise up a highway for Him Who rides through the deserts, By His Name *Yah*, And exult before Him." Your Bible probably spells it "JAH," but remember the letter "J" did not come into use until the 16th century. Yah is the short form of Yahweh. For the translators to use His correct Name only *once* out of *6,823* times makes me question their motivation. I smell a rat! How about you?

Here's a dictionary definition of god: **1)** any of various beings conceived of as supernatural and immortal; esp., a male deity, **2)** an idol, **3)** a person or thing deified, **4) [G-]** in monotheistic religions, the creator and ruler of the universe; Supreme Being.

In the Thesaurus under "god" (lower case "g"), 48 pagan gods are listed and if their double names are counted there are 64. Under "God" (upper case "G") the Thesaurus lists **1)** [The Judeo-Christian deity] Lord, Jehovah, Yahweh and then 53 descriptive titles are listed. **2)** [The supreme deity of other religions] Allah (Islam); Brahma (Hinduism); Buddha (Buddhism); Mazda or Ormazd (Zoroastrianism).

The above definition was taken from Webster's New World Dictionary and Thesaurus, Second Edition, Copyright 2002. Now you can see how all the (gods, Gods) are lumped together.

What's In A Name?

The 11th edition of the Encyclopedia Britannica states this definition: "GOD – the common Teutonic word for a personal object of worship . . . applied to all those superhuman beings of the heathen mythologies. The word 'god' on the conversion of the Teutonic races to Christianity was adopted as the name of the one Supreme Being . . ."

It was *adopted*! Need I say more?

I find it curious that the Yahudim (Jews) built a fence around His Name and declared that it was too sacred to be pronounced *and the English translators went along with it (even though it was a "Jewish" tradition)*. However, everything else in the Scriptures that the Church has deemed "Jewish" (when it really isn't) is disregarded like the Sabbath, Feast Days, Dietary Laws, etc. But the **NON-USE** of the Creator's name seemed to be just fine, leaving us with a POWER SHORTAGE.

At least, during that time, the Yahudim (Jews) had a pretty good reason...*fear of death*...for not using the Name. Because of severe persecution, the Yisra'elites (Israelites) stopped using the Name except for the High Priest who would speak it once a year during Yom Kippur – The Day of Atonement. What excuse does the "Church" have? There's no doubt in my mind; it has been the work of the evil one.

Let's look at the word "Lord." Ironically, Lord means BAAL in Hebrew (see Strong's #01168). "They think the dreams they tell one another (made-up words, substitutions) will make My people forget My Name, just as their fathers forgot My Name through

BAAL (LORD)" (Yirmeyahu [Jeremiah] 23:27). In chapter 2, verse 8b we see "...the prophets prophesied by Ba'al, and walked after *matters* that did not profit."

The Westminster Desk Dictionary of the English Language defines "lord" as: "**1)** a person who has dominion over others, as a feudal superior, **2)** a person who is a leader in a profession, **3)** a titled nobleman or peer, as in Great Britain, **4)** Lords, See House of Lords, **5)** (cap) God or Jehovah, **6)** (cap) the Savior, Jesus Christ. – v.t.**7)** lord it over, to domineer over."

The Church calls upon the name, magnifies the name, glorifies the name, but they actually do not use The Name because they've been taught to use the title *Lord*. The closest the Church comes to using His Name is when they say, "Hallelu<u>Yah</u>," which means praise Yah the short form of Yahweh.

Don't get all bent out of shape if you're hearing this for the first time. Yahweh is certainly smarter than we are and He already knew we'd bring His Name into non-use. He has it all under control. He's restoring it in this hour.

You can start using His real Name now or you will for sure be using it later. *(Resistance is futile.)* Here's why...

Hosea 2:17 states, "And I shall remove the names of the Ba'als from her mouth, and they shall no more be remembered by their name." Again, Ba'al means "lord" in Hebrew and it doesn't matter if you capitalize the first letter or the whole word or put a dash in between it; the spelling, pronunciation and meaning are the same.

What's In A Name?

Can we really have an intimate relationship with someone if we don't know their name? Let's get back to loving Him the way He wants to be loved. Using His Name is one of the ways we can show our love.

In Yahanan (John) 17:6-7 Yahshua says, "I have revealed Your Name to the men whom You (Yahweh) gave Me (Yahshua) out of the world. They were Yours, and You gave them to Me, and they have guarded Your Word." In verses 25 and 26 He says, "O righteous Father, indeed the world did not know You, but I knew You, and these knew that You sent Me. And I have made **Your Name** known to them, and shall make it known, so that the love with which You loved Me might be in them, and I in them."

Even the ROCKS are starting to cry out thanks to archaeological finds. On the Ossuary (bone box) of Ya'akob (James) the inscription reads "Ya'akob son of Yosef brother of Y'shua" [first witness]. And the Dead Sea Scrolls show the Father's name YHWH [second witness]. In addition, the Moabite Stone, dated around 930 BC. reveals YHWH's name in Ancient Hebrew Script [third witness].

There are 6,832 compelling reasons to use His Hebrew Name. It's in His Word that many times. Not everyone agrees on the exact spelling or pronunciation, but we know for sure that our Savior's Name is not "Jesus," "God" or "Lord." If we are trying with our whole heart to please our Creator and Savior, I believe He will accept our sincere efforts and that His Rauch ha Kodesh (Holy Spirit) will lead us into all Truth.

Let Yahshua Rock Your World

More about names:

One of the most UN-interesting parts of the Scripture for me has always been the genealogies. You know So-n-So begat So-n-So and he begat So-n-So, etc., etc., etc. BORING! Right? Well, I've learned that there are treasures in the Hebrew Names even in the genealogies.

I'm telling you, our Father is so awesome that the more I learn of Him and His ways the more humble I am. As a matter of fact, when a person starts to search for His treasures in the Hebrew language and read His Word from a Hebraic perspective, it's like sitting under a spout that's gushing more water than one can contain. It reminds me of the Scripture in Ezekiel, chapter forty-seven where the water is flowing from the temple: First it was ankle-deep, then it was knee-deep, then waist-deep, then it was a river deep enough to swim in, a river that could not be passed through.

I don't know if you remember the TV show Hogan's Heroes. Well, the more I learn, the more I feel like Schultz: *"I KNOW NOTHING"!!!*

Let's get back to the importance of Hebrew names in the Scriptures. Keep in mind that every letter (every jot, every tittle) has meaning and we're commanded not to *add to* or *take away from* His Word.

Remember all those "begats" in the genealogy of Adam? Well I found out through Pastor Mark Biltz that the Hebrew meanings of the names in that genealogy spell out Yahweh's plan of redemption. Take a look below:

What's In A Name?

Adam	=	Mankind is
Seth	=	Appointed to
Enosh	=	Feeble, Frail, Mortality
Canaan	=	A Fixed Dwelling Place
MaHalaliel	=	Elohim Who is Praised
Yared	=	To Come Down or Descend
Enoch	=	Walk with Elohim (Train is Enoch in Hebrew)
Methuselah	=	A Man Sent Forth
Lamed	=	To be Beaten, Smitten or Tortured
Noah	=	The One Who Brought Rest

Mankind is appointed to feeble, frail mortality, a fixed dwelling place. Elohim Who is praised comes down to instruct. A man sent forth to be beaten smitten or tortured bring rest – a quiet peace. (Biltz, Mark. Audio Torah Parsha B'reisheet. "In the Beginning." 6 Oct 2007. www.elshaddaiministries.us/audio/torah5768/20071006t1breisheet.html.)

There is much buried treasure in the Scriptures – we just have to be willing to dig through the layers of tradition and uncover the ROCK!

"Therefore My people shall know My Name, in that day, for I am the One Who is speaking. See, it is I."
(Isaiah 52:6)

"And it shall be that everyone who calls on the Name of Yahweh shall be delivered…"
(Joel 2:32)

> "Remember the Sabbath day, to set it apart. Six days you labour, and shall do all your work, but the seventh day is a Sabbath of Yahweh your Elohim. You do not do any work – you, nor your son, nor your daughter, nor your male servant, nor your female servant, nor your cattle, nor your stranger who is within your gates. For in six days Yahweh made the heavens and the earth, the sea, and all that is in them, and rested the seventh day. Therefore Yahweh blessed the Sabbath day and set it apart."
> (Exodus 20:8-11)

Chapter 4: Sabbath

Although I thought I was keeping *all ten* of the Ten Commandments, I found out that I was breaking the first four BIG TIME. The first four Commandments define our relationship with Elohim, how we are to worship Him, love Him and obey Him; and the last six define our relationship with our fellow man.

In this chapter we're going to focus on the Fourth Commandment regarding the Sabbath. The Hebrew word for Sabbath is Shabbath and it means "rest, to cease, to pause or take an intermission." On the Sabbath we are to take the day off from our regular activities and devote our time and attention to our Creator. Think of it as a vacation day with Elohim. Wow!

Early in my Christian walk I was curious about a lot of things I read in the Scriptures that were not being taught in the Church. One of those things was the Sabbath (the seventh day). I was taught that the Sabbath was for the Yahudim (Jews) and since the New Covenant is for Christians we worship on Sunday – the day Christ arose. Sadly, this is not what Scripture teaches. But *hearing* these same teachings year after year, I developed faith to believe they were true. After all, these pastors and teachers were learned men and women with degrees and years of experience in ministry. *(I thought to myself, "Surely they know the truth.")*

While I'm disappointed about what I was taught, I'm not being accusatory because this deception has been around for centuries and it is only by Elohim's grace and mercy that these ROCKS are being unearthed during this time period as we approach the end of the age. Don't blame your pastor or your favorite TV preacher. They are only teaching what has been dispensed to them from the "so called" institutions of higher learning, better known as seminaries.

As far as the notion that the Sabbath is for the Yahudim (Jews), it turns out that the Sabbath was instituted in the very beginning before there was even a Yahudi (Jew) of the tribe of Yahuda (Judah) and it was given as a gift to mankind. So, when I discovered that it was the Roman emperor Constantine, operating through the Catholic Church, who changed the worship day from the seventh day to the first day of the week – *I was mortified.*

In Constantine's decree March 7, 321 A.D. he stated, "On the venerable day of the Sun let the magistrates and people residing in cities rest, and let all workshops be closed." And in A.D. 325 he wrote, "Let us then have nothing in common with the detestable Jewish crowd: for we have received from our Savior a different way … Strive and pray continually that the purity of your soul may not seem in anything to be sullied by fellowship with the customs of these most wicked men … All should unite in desiring that which

Sabbath

sound reason appears to demand and in avoiding all participation in the perjured conduct of the Jews." *(Can you feel the love?)*

Yes, a mere, mortal man changed the day that the Creator of the Universe sanctified and made Holy (Set-Apart) – the day that El Shaddai commanded us to keep. You can research this historical fact for yourself. In the 1876 book, "The Faith of Our Fathers," James Cardinal Gibbons, the Catholic Archbishop of Baltimore, agreed the shift to Sunday was **not** based on the Bible, but was solely the work of the Catholic Church.

Once I swallowed that pill, which felt more like a ROCK than a pill, I thought it was the last one I'd have to swallow, but little did I know many more were on the way. We'll investigate other rocks later in the book.

For now, we'll continue with the Sabbath. As I said before, I was naturally curious about why Christians worshipped on Sunday instead of the Sabbath. The thought may have crossed your mind as well since the word "Sabbath" appears 137 times in the King James Version of the Bible, and the word "Sunday" is absent though "first day of the week" occurs eight times.

Interestingly, while most Bible versions use the phrase "first day of the week" in Acts 20:7a, a 1990 word-for-word translation of the same Scripture by Greek experts Robert K. Brown and Philip W. Comfort in the New Greek English Interlinear New Covenant from Tyndale House Publishers, actually renders it as "one of the Sabbaths."

Let Yahshua Rock Your World

Here are some examples of how the Sabbath has been explained away by many well-meaning teachers and preachers:

1. The Sabbath was for the Yahudim (Jews) and since the New Covenant is for Christians, we worship on Sunday. *(Curiously, the first century Renewed / New Covenant believers – Yahudim (Jews) and Greeks kept the Sabbath on the seventh day. See Acts 18:4.)*
2. Yahshua (Jesus) rose from the dead on Sunday and that's why we worship Him on Sunday. *(Not true. He was crucified on Wednesday and rose on Saturday at the close of the Sabbath. There are numerous sources that support this truth. Even the Companion Bible gets it right on page 170, Appendix 144; on page 172, Appendix 148; and pages 179-182 Appendix 156. A Biblical day is from evening to evening so the first day of the week technically begins on Saturday evening after sundown.)*
3. The disciples broke bread on the first day of the week so that's the day the Church worships Him (Acts 20:7-8, 11). *(According to Acts 2:46, the disciples met from house to house and broke bread daily – it was their custom – so there is no basis for picking out a Scripture which isn't even talking about the Sabbath to use to support this false teaching. In Matthew 6:11 the disciples were taught to pray for their <u>daily</u> bread.)*
4. Another Scripture that has been used to promote the idea that the Sabbath was changed to Sunday is 1 Corinthians 16:2, where Paul directed the Corinthians to take up a

Sabbath

collection every week for the poor in Jerusalem on the "first day of the week" and he would stop on his way to Jerusalem to collect it. *(Let's take a closer look. Who was this gift for? It was for the poor Saints in Jerusalem, not for Yahweh's work of spreading the Gospel or for some other Church program. We're not told how many weeks they were to set their gifts aside; but Paul's travel in this instance appears to be for a specific occasion and not a permanent policy. The Sabbath is not mentioned in this passage and the first day of the week technically starts at sundown on Saturday evening after the Sabbath according to Biblical reckoning of days. In the Complete Jewish Bible the first day of the week is rendered: Motza'ei-Shabbat which means "going out of Shabbat.")*

5. Finally, some say that Yahshua spoke on all the Commandments except the Fourth Commandment, and therefore it does not apply. *(This is not true. Yahshua spoke repeatedly about the Sabbath in Matthew 12. He gave instructions on how to keep it, stating in verse 12 "...it is right to do good on the Sabbath." The first century Gentile believers rested on the Sabbath just as they always had.)*

Unfortunately, many believers (myself included) have been led astray by such interpretations. I accepted these explanations as truth for many years without searching the Scriptures for myself. So just imagine how that ROCK felt going down my throat when I had to swallow the fact I had been breaking the Fourth Commandment for more than twenty-five years. It was like an earthquake – it shook me to the core. *I did not know what I did not know.*

Returning to Constantine, not only did he have the arrogance to change the day of worship, he changed it to the day that pagans worship the sun – Sunday *(see Appendix 2).*

Doesn't it just stand to reason that if Yahweh said, "This is the day that I want you to worship Me," that Satan would pervert that day to the day that he is worshipped?

Let's look at what day the Scriptures *(not men)* teach is the Sabbath. Elohim Himself, the Creator and King of the Universe, sanctified the seventh day and made it Holy (Set-Apart). "Remember the Sabbath day, to set it apart. Six days you labour, and shall do all your work, but the **seventh day** is a Sabbath of Yahweh your Elohim" (Exodus 20:8-9). Verse 11 reads, "For in six days Yahweh made the heavens and the earth, the sea, and all that is in them, and rested the **seventh day**. Therefore Yahweh blessed the Sabbath day and set it apart."

Throughout the Scriptures, starting at Genesis, the Sabbath has always been the seventh day and it *never* changed! Here's an exercise you can do which proves my point. Just read the Book of Acts and circle the Sabbath every time you see it and you'll find that it's jammed packed with the Sabbath. You will have to *hop, skip* and *jump* around the text to avoid the Sabbath.

It truly is amazing how effective "false doctrine" can be. Once you've been conditioned (brainwashed) into believing the Sabbath does not apply to you then when you see the word in your Bible,

Sabbath

your mind becomes dull, your eyes gloss over and you become hard of hearing. Man made traditions set like cement, making it difficult for truth to penetrate.

In 2001, Jan Marcussen, author of *National Sunday Law*, was so sure there was no Bible verse declaring the first day to be the Sabbath that he offered up $1 million for clear, Scriptural proof. He responded in March 2008 to *WorldNetDaily*, "I didn't get even one response claiming the $1 million from any theologian, bishop, cardinal, pope or anyone else. Why not? Because they can't. [Observing Sunday as the Sabbath] is the biggest hoax the world has ever seen."

Do your research and you'll find that the Catholic Church even boasts about having authority to change the day of worship from Saturday / Sabbath to Sunday / Sun-god (Mithras) day. For instance, The Kansas City Catholic wrote on Feb. 9, 1893 "The Catholic Church of its own infallible authority created Sunday a holy day to take the place of the Sabbath of the old law." In one statement when the church leadership was asked how they knew they had authority to change the day, the answer in so many words was "we must have had authority, because we were able to do it."

You may not realize this but millions of people were killed so that change could be instituted. Torture and murder were methods the Church used to do it. Sabbath-keepers were definitely in the line of fire. *(Ever heard of the inquisition or the crusades?)*

The truth is Yahshua was given *all* authority not the Catholic Church. He could have changed the day of worship if He had wanted to but He did not because He only did what His Father told Him to do and His Father didn't tell Him to do it!

Is the seventh day important? YES, YES, a thousand times YES! Here are some reasons why:

It was given to commemorate creation and shows outwardly who we worship as our Creator – "For in six days Yahweh made the heavens and the earth, the sea, and all that is in them, and rested the seventh day." (Exodus 20:11) "…worship Him who made the heaven and the earth, and sea, and fountains of water" (Revelation 14:7b). *If we don't honor Him as Creator on the Sabbath, we might as well join the evolutionists who believe everything started with a "big bang."*

It's included in the Ten Commandments – "Remember the Sabbath day, to set it apart. Six days you labour, and shall do all your work, but the seventh day is a Sabbath of Yahweh your Elohim…" (Exodus 20:8-10). *He wrote it with His own finger and told us to remember it and keep it Holy* (Deuteronomy 9:10).

It's how we delight in Him – "If you do turn back your foot from the Sabbath, from doing your pleasure on My Set-Apart day, and shall call the Sabbath 'a delight,' the Set-Apart day of Yahweh 'esteemed,' and shall esteem it, not doing your own ways, nor finding your own pleasure, nor speaking your own words, then you shall delight yourself in Yahweh" (Isaiah 58:13-14a).

We are blessed for keeping it – "…Blessed is the man who does this…guarding the Sabbath lest he profane it, and guarding his hand from doing any evil" (Isaiah 56:2).

It's in the future – not just in the past – "So there remains a Shabbat-keeping for Elohim's people" (Hebrews 4:9).

It's a way to show our obedience – "Let us therefore do our utmost to enter into that rest, lest anyone fall after the same example of disobedience" (Hebrews 4:10-11).

It's the day Yahweh blessed and made Holy – "Therefore Yahweh blessed the Sabbath day and set it apart" (Exodus 20:11b).

It's the only day in Scripture given a special name – *The first six days had no name; they were given ordinal numbers – first day, second day, third day, etc., but the seventh day was given a unique name. In Hebrew, it's "Shabbat," meaning "rest, to cease, to pause or take an intermission." In English, the word is "Sabbath."*

Yahweh set the seventh day apart for man to fellowship with Him – "The Sabbath was made for man" (Mark 2:27). *In creation Elohim made man on the sixth day and made the Sabbath for man on the seventh day.*

Yahshua kept the Sabbath – "And He came to Natsareth (Nazareth), where He had been brought up. And according to His practice, He went into the congregation on the Sabbath day, and stood up to read" (Luke 4:16).

It was also Paul's custom to keep the Sabbath – "…And according to his practice, Sha'ul (Paul) went in unto them, and for three Sabbaths was reasoning with them from the Scriptures…" (Acts 17:2). *Neither Paul nor any of the other disciples ever taught people to come back the next day for a Sunday (1st day of the week) service.*

The Disciples Kept the Sabbath 85 Times in the book of Acts – (see *Appendix 3*).

Both Yahudim (Jews) and Greeks kept the Sabbath – "And he [Paul] was reasoning in the congregation every Sabbath, and won over both Yahudim (Jews) and Greeks" (Acts 18:4).

It is for the foreigner as well as the home born – "Also the sons of the foreigner who join themselves to Yahweh, to be His servants, all who guard the Sabbath, and not profane it, and hold fast to My Covenant – them I shall bring to My Set-Apart

Mountain, and let them rejoice in My House of prayer..." (Isaiah 56:6-7). *The word for foreigner in Hebrew is "nakar" which means one who is a stranger to the ways of Yahweh, often called a heathen or gentile.*

Here's what happened when Paul and Barnabas were in Antioch – "And on the next Sabbath **almost all the city came** together to hear the Word of Elohim" (Acts 13:44). *You'll notice it reads "the next Sabbath." Why didn't Paul simply say come back tomorrow [Sunday] to learn more, rather than wait an entire week for the next Sabbath to arrive?*

It's a sign (mark) between Elohim and His people – "Between Me and the children of Yisra'ěl (Israel) it is a sign forever" (Exodus 31:17). *The Hebrew word for sign is owt which means "a mark or a proof." It's the same word used in Genesis 9:12-17 for the sign of the rainbow. If you have received Yahshua as your Savior then you are grafted into the olive tree and have become a member of the commonwealth of Israel. You are His bride and the Sabbath is a sign, "A MARK OF PROOF," that you belong to Him.*

Keeping the Sabbath is not optional – it is a command – "Remember the Sabbath day, to set it apart" (Exodus 20:8). *When Yahshua said,*

"...teaching them to observe all that I have commanded you" in Matthew 28:20, He was referring to the Tanakh (Old Covenant) because the B'rit Hadasha (New Covenant) was not written at that time. This truth alone ROCKED my boat. It's impossible to get a clear understanding of the Scriptures by starting in the Book of John. The Scriptures must be read as a whole to avoid misinterpretations. The New Covenant is jam packed with references to the Old Covenant. In one translation of the "New Covenant" [which is about ¼ of the whole Bible], there are 627 references to the "Old Covenant" (see Appendix 4). Are you thinking what I'm thinking? That it might be wise to find out what's in the beginning of the Book. After all, Isaiah 46:10 says the end is declared out of the beginning.

The Sabbath is to be observed during the future reign of Yahshua – Isaiah 66:22-23 reads, "For as the new heavens and the new earth that I make stand before Me, declares Yahweh, so your seed and your name shall stand. And it shall be that from New Moon to New Moon, and from Sabbath to Sabbath, <u>all flesh</u> shall come to worship before Me, declares Yahweh." *Again, resistance is futile! It's in your future – why not make it a part of your life today?*

Hear me on this; the Sabbath is a *"REALLY BIG DEAL"* to Yahweh. While it's <u>not</u> a salvation issue it is an obedience issue.

Sabbath

Once we are saved we're supposed to obey. He made the Sabbath for man (mankind) not just for a particular people. He sanctified it and made it Holy (Set-Apart). It is not like any other day of the week. Sun-god-day worship is not the day He chose, but the day that a mortal man chose for the sole purpose of bringing the pagans and the Christians together in order to control both groups.

Look up the word Syncretism in your dictionary. Yahshua said He would rather we be cold or hot – not lukewarm (a mixture of cold and hot). We are not to mix the Holy with the profane and He made the Sabbath Holy – *it's just that simple.*

So why is it that today most who confess "Jesus is Lord" don't follow His example? The truth is the "father of lies," "the god of this present world" has influenced us to ignore, avoid and reason our way around keeping the Sabbath.

History shows that it was almost 300 years after Messiah's ministry on earth before the majority of the Christian Church rejected the Sabbath. The enemy always wants to pervert the pure, true worship of Yahweh and his indoctrination has been very successful. Just as he did in the garden with Eve, he is still asking, "Has God said..." And he is saying things like, "What's so special about the Sabbath; you should worship God every day or any day you choose."

Constantine chose Sunday – himself a pagan worshipper who "supposedly" adopted Christianity. *(Let me interrupt myself here and remind you that anyone can say they are a Christian, but you will know them by their fruit – you have to become a fruit inspector and from the research I've read about Constantine after his "so called" conversion, his fruit was rotten to the core.* **He had his wife and eldest son killed *after* his conversion and wasn't baptized until 16 years later on his death bed. Beyond that, he retained the title and the dignity of a Pontifex Maximus, or high priest of the heathen hierarchy and his coins bore on the one side**

his image and on the other side the figure of the Sun god with the inscription: "committed to the invincible sun.")
Hold on now before you accuse me of being judgmental – he may have repented and received the Messiah on his death bed – but his fruit up to that point would qualify him as a "wolf in sheep's clothing." Besides, the apostles exposed false teaching and we should too (see Matthew 7:15-16).

At the council of Laodicea in 363, the Church of Rome (Roman Catholic Church) declared: "Christians must not judaize by resting on the Sabbath, but must work on that day, rather honoring the Lords' Day [Sunday]; and, if they can, resting then as Christians. But if any shall be found to be judaizers, let them be anathema from Christ." *Wait just a minute, wasn't Yahshua (Jesus) a Yahudi (Jew) and Paul as well? This sounds like anti-Semitism personified!*

Yes, most are worshiping on the wrong day because "the deceiver of the whole world" is in our midst stealthily hiding the truth in plain view (see Revelation 12:9 and 1 John 5:19). His deception has been very successful. How can I say this? Because Christians don't keep the Sabbath any more.

Sabbath

Yet, you can search the Scriptures from Genesis to Revelation and you will not find a single verse that says His Sabbath was changed to a different day or that a day begins at midnight instead of at sundown. Understanding Biblical reckoning of evening and morning is imperative because this single "cover up" has led many to an incorrect conclusion about the Sabbath. There is not a single verse, not one, that tells us that the Ten Commandments are for the Yahudim (Jews) and are not to be kept. In fact, the Scriptures declare the seventh day to be the Sabbath throughout the entire Bible.

Other Scriptures used most often by the Church to show that Paul rejected the Sabbath are found in Galatians, Romans and Colossians.

We'll start with Galatians

Paul says in Galatians 4:9-10, "….how do you turn again to the weak and poor elementary matters, to which you wish to be enslaved again? You observe *days* and *months* and *seasons* and *years*." On the surface (where the Western mindset lives) it appears that he is criticizing the Sabbath, but when you dig a little deeper, you'll find some very interesting facts.

Let's start at Verse 8. "But then, indeed, not knowing Elohim, you served those which by nature are not mighty ones." *In case you didn't catch that, they had been serving pagan idols.* Verse 9 starts out with, "But now after you have known Elohim…" *These are people who are just coming into the faith. Then it goes on to say,* "…or rather are known by Elohim…" *According to Matthew 7:21, the people who are known by God are those who do the will of the Father – they keep His Commandments.*

Then Paul asks in Galatians 4:9, "….how do you turn again to the weak and poor elementary matters, to which you wish to be enslaved again?" *I hope you can see that what they were turning back to was their former idolatrous pagan practices.* Paul couldn't have been condemning the Sabbath because it was not part of these idolatrous practices and you can't turn again to that which you never observed.

So in Verse 10 when Paul condemns them for observing "days" and "months" and "seasons" and "years," he is talking about something totally different from the Sabbath. Without understanding the history, culture and background of Galatia at that time, it would be impossible to figure out exactly what Paul was saying.

Galatia was part of the Roman Empire, in which observances and practices honoring pagan gods were attached to virtually every day, season, month and year. For instance, the first day of the week was devoted to the sun god. The first month of the year was devoted to Janus, the god of beginnings, from which January is named. The spring season was devoted to the goddess Cybele and her male partner, Attis, in honor of whom a joyous spring resurrection festival was celebrated. Paul was pinpointing these idolatrous practices the Galatians had observed when they "did not know God." He was not criticizing them for Sabbath-keeping or observing Biblical Festivals.

Sabbath

Let's go to Romans

Romans 14:5-6 is a verse that has been used to teach that it is alright to worship Elohim any day of the week meaning that the Sabbath is no more important than any other day. "One indeed judges one day above another, another judges every day *alike*. Let each one be completely persuaded in his own mind. He who minds the day, minds it to Yahweh…"

But if you read Romans 14 in context you'll see that it's talking about food – fasting and vegetarianism. The congregation in Rome included Yahudim (Jews) and Gentiles with different eating and fasting practices that were not found in Scripture which became a point of contention. Some of the religious Yahudim (Jews) chose to "fast twice a week," while the custom of some of the gentiles from a Roman background was to "avoid meats" on some days.

So Paul was expressing the fact that those who fasted certain times of the week or those who abstained from meats on particular days of the week both gave thanks to Elohim on those days. He was not talking about Sabbath-keeping at all.

Finally let's look at Colossians

Colossians 2:16-17 reads, "Let no one therefore judge you in eating or in drinking, or in respect of a festival or a new moon or Sabbaths – which are a shadow of what is to come." Some conclude that this verse proves that Paul rejected the Sabbath and Festival observances. But wait a minute, eating and drinking is mentioned in this verse as well as the Sabbath. Was Paul rejecting eating and drinking? Let's take a deeper look and find out what's really going on here.

Let Yahshua Rock Your World

What was Paul really addressing? This letter was written "to the Set-Apart ones in Colosse" (Colossians 1:2). History shows that asceticism was creeping into the assembly. Asceticism is defined as: to train the body; self-denying; austere; one who leads a life of strict self-denial, esp. for religious purposes. Promoters of this heresy criticized and condemned anything pleasurable. *(In today's vernacular they might be called self-righteous, holier than thou, sanctimonious snobs.)*

Paul was combating this heresy by encouraging the faithful brothers at Colossae not to let anyone judge them in their obedience to Yahweh in eating and drinking and in keeping the Sabbaths, New Moon, and Festivals *(which by the way are festive and joyous occasions)*. You'll also notice in verse 17 these **"are"** not **"were"** a shadow of things to come. They are bridal rehearsals for our wedding day. Oh taste and see that Yahweh is good!

Summary

The seventh day is the Sabbath all over the world *(see Appendix 5)*. The Sabbath was the first day of man's existence and if Elohim rested on the seventh day of creation and set it apart, Adam would have rested on that day also. Yahweh created this day for man for a day of rest and fellowship with Him – it's a gift from our loving Creator. The Sabbath is not a salvation issue, it's an obedience issue.

It would be one thing if Yahweh had not given us instructions to follow, but He did. He told us in His Word how to worship Him – *Do His Commandments* (Revelation 22:14).

Sabbath

Can you imagine what would happen if the Church actually started following His instructions? "Denominationalism," "Dispensationalism," and the "Doctrine of Demons" would cease. No longer would we tell Elohim when to meet with us but we would let Him tell us when to meet with Him. If you believe that's the way it should be, you will be challenged to find out more about keeping the Sabbath.

Initially, I struggled and stumbled while trying to obey this ROCK of Truth. After all, the whole world is set for Sunday. But when I learned that the Sabbath was an outward sign, a mark if you will, of those who are His, it hit me like a BOULDER! Now, I look forward to His Sabbath!

It's His Divine appointment with His bride – a rehearsal for the final wedding. In addition, it shows the world who we are betrothed to. So knowing this truth, I had to choose whether or not I was going to obey Yahweh or man. Would I meet Him at the end of the age on **"that day"** and say, "I went to Church every Sunday (morning and evening), on Wednesday nights and daily during the Church's revival?" And will He respond, *"I never knew you?"*

"And you, speak to the children of Yisra'ĕl, saying, 'My *Sabbaths* you are to guard, by all means, for it is a sign between Me and you throughout your generations, to know that I, Yahweh, am setting you apart."
Exodus 31:13

> "And He said, If you diligently obey the voice of Yahweh your Elohim and do what is right in His eyes, and shall listen to His commands and shall guard all His laws, I shall bring on you none of the diseases I brought on the Mitsrites, for I am Yahweh who heals you."
> (Exodus 15:26

Chapter 5:
It's The Law

Are you "under the law" or are you "in the Law"?

"And then I shall declare to them,
I never knew you, depart from Me,
you who work <u>lawlessness</u>!" Matthew 7:23

Before you start to hemorrhage, tighten your seatbelt and hang on because we're going to the ROCK quarry again to find out what it really means to be "under the law" or "in the Law." It may not be what you think.

Perhaps more than with any other subject in the Bible, the enemy has had a field day with the Law – he has literally wreaked havoc in the Church with this one.

From the youngest age (about 8 or 9 years old), I can vividly remember walking to a neighbor's house with my sisters, just a couple of blocks away from our home, to attend summer Bible school – that's where I learned the Ten Commandments. During that era, the Ten Commandments were displayed everywhere: in the schools, at the court house, and even in the Church.

Let Yahshua Rock Your World

Now let's fast forward about forty years. I turned the Television on one day and a popular preacher from a mega-Church in California was preaching on the Ten Commandments and the Law and I could hardly believe what I was hearing. *(He had so much passion in his delivery that I could almost see veins popping out on his forehead.)* When he said, "You don't have to keep the Ten Commandments anymore because we're no longer under the Law but under grace," you could have knocked me over with a feather I was so stunned.

Since that encounter, I've heard many preachers and teachers make similar statements with plenty of Scripture to back them up.

But what I've learned is the seeds that have gotten us off track were planted centuries ago. The problem stems from the fact that without an understanding of the structure of Yahudi (Jewish) law, the Hebrew culture, the context of Paul's teachings and where the text was mistranslated or poorly translated in our English Bibles, then it may seem that Paul was contradicting himself.

After all Paul says some very positive things about the Law:

> "The Torah [Law] is Spiritual" (Romans 7:14).

> "...the Torah [Law] truly is Set-Apart, and the Command Set-Apart, and righteous, and good" (Romans 7:12).

> "I delight in the Torah [Law] of Elohim according to the inward man..." (Romans 7:22).

"I myself truly serve the Torah [Law] of Elohim..." (Romans 7:25).

"For not the hearers of the Torah [Law] are righteous in the sight of Elohim, but the doers of the Law shall be declared right" (Romans 2:13).

"...we establish the Torah [Law]" (Romans 3:31).

"For the Torah of the Spirit of the life in Messiah Yahshua has set me free from the Law of sin and of death" (Romans 8:2).

"For even as you did present your members as servants of uncleanness, and of lawlessness resulting in lawlessness, so now present your members as servants of righteousness resulting in Set-Apartness" (Romans 6:19).

"For whatever was written before was written for our instruction [Torah], that through endurance and encouragement of the Scriptures [Old Covenant] we might have the expectation" (Romans 15:4).

"The circumcision is naught [nothing], and the uncircumcision is naught [nothing], but the guarding of the Commands of Elohim *does matter!*" (1 Corinthians 7:19).

"...and all were immersed into Mosheh [Torah] in the cloud and in the sea, and all ate the same spiritual food, and all drank the same spiritual drink. For they drank of that spiritual ROCK that followed, and the ROCK was Messiah" (1 Corinthians 10:2-4).

"Is the Torah then against the promises of Elohim? Let it not be!" (Galatians 3:21).

"For the secret of lawlessness [Torahlessness] is already at work" (2 Thessalonians 2:7).

"…and that from a babe you have known the Set-Apart Scriptures [Tanakh], which are able to make you wise for deliverance through belief in Messiah Yahshua…" (2 Timothy 3:15).

"All Scripture [Torah] is breathed by Elohim and profitable for teaching, for reproof, for setting straight, for instruction in righteousness…" (2 Timothy 3:16).

All of the above verses shed a positive light on the Law. But you can find just as many verses that appear to show that Paul was teaching against the Law. What's going on here? Let's remove some of the top soil and dig deeper into the ROCK.

To begin with, there are many facets to the word "law" that are missed in the English translations. So if you use a broad brush stroke, you'll have some significant interpretation problems. For instance, the word translated "law" in the New Covenant can refer to:

It's The Law

- The Mosaic Covenant
- Five Books of Moses
- The entire Tanakh (Torah, Prophets and the Writings)
- A specific Biblical Command
- A Principle
- Legalism
- Parallel concepts of flesh or works – self-effort

Here's another issue: The best Greek word the translators could come up with for the Torah *(1st five books of the Bible)* was Nomos which simply means "law." As Brad Scott (a Hebrew Roots teacher) would say, "It could mean good laws, bad laws, crazy laws, strange laws or stupid laws." And so we're stuck with the English word "law," with its negative connotation. [**I fought the law and the law won.**]

But in Hebrew the word "Torah" means *"**utterance, teaching, instruction** or **revelation**"* from Elohim and derives from the stem "yara" which means "to shoot or **throw**." Therefore, the Torah aims and points us in the right direction through instruction and moves us in that direction. Can you see how different the Hebrew meaning is?

Peter warned that we would have difficulty understanding some of Paul's teachings because we are unlearned (2 Peter 3:16).

Here are some definitions of the phrases associated with the law from the Greek:

Upo nomon is Greek for "under law," - to pervert the Torah into a legalistic system for working out one's own righteousness / salvation. Those who were "under the law" were people burdened in a legalistic perspective of the Torah better known as the "Oral Torah," which embodies man made ordinances and restrictions. (This will become crystal clear when we discuss the structure of Jewish law.)

Anomos is Greek for anti-Torah – **1)** destitute of (the Mosaic) law; a) of the Gentiles; **2)** departing from the law, a violator of the law, lawless wicked.

Ennomos is Greek for in-lawed or in the Torah – **1)** bound to the law, **2)** bound by the law, lawful, and **3)** lawful, regular.

This example might help you distinguish between *upo nomon* "under the law," *anomos* "without the Law," and *ennomos* "in the Law."

> If someone is *"under the law,"* that person is following some man-made doctrines [not found in Scripture], or the letter of the law written on stone instead of the Spirit of the Law written on their heart, or some legalistic interpretation that goes beyond the Torah [as in Rabbinic Judaism]. Someone who is *anti-Torah* either doesn't know about the Torah [as is the case of most Gentiles] or believes it does not apply to them [like most Christians]. Those considered *"in the Law,"* follow the Torah in the Spirit of Yahshua. They walk as

> He walked - keeping His Sabbath, His Dietary Laws, and His Festivals and they use His real Name, with a truly converted heart (see Deuteronomy 5:29).

Here's a practical, modern-day example of being "under the law:"

> If I'm driving my car and I run a red light, then I'm under the law, i.e., under the BURDEN of the law. I will have to pay the fine that's established by the legal system regardless of the cost. But if someone comes along and pays the fine / penalty for me and I accept the gift with the understanding that I will wait for those green lights in the future, then I'm operating "in the law."

Beyond the different definitions of the Law, there are issues with inaccurate translations. Look at this verse in the KJV as opposed to the original Greek manuscripts.

> Romans 3:19, "Now we know that what things soever the Law saith, it saith to them who are under the law: that every mouth may be stopped, and all the world may become guilty before God" (KJV).

Yet, the Greek manuscripts do not convey this meaning at all.

The English phrase translated "under the law" here should read "in the Law," for the Greek text reads en to nomo, not upo nomon ("under law"). This verse addresses the question, to whom does the Torah speak? **Contrary to the KJV, the Torah does not speak to those who are "under the law."**

It's important to catch this difference because it will clarify some of the innocent misinterpretations that the Western Church has made that have kept us from worshipping our Creator in Spirit and in Truth. The correct translation shows that the Torah speaks to those who live within its boundaries – those who are "in the Law." The phrase "under the law" refers to those who have perverted the pure Law of Elohim into some legalistic burden that no one can keep and should not be used in this verse.

The following example shows yet another issue with one translation rendering "under the law" incorrectly and the other rendering it correctly:

The NIV shows Romans 2:12 as:

> "All who sin apart from the Law will also perish apart from the Law, and all who sin <u>under the law</u> will be judged by the Law."

However, the KJV, in this case more accurately has:

> "For as many as have sinned without Law shall also perish without Law: and as many as have sinned <u>in the Law</u> shall be judged by the Law."

The NIV uses the phrase "under the law," yet the Greek text clearly reads *en nomo* meaning, "in Law," not *upo nomon*, meaning "under law."

With such poor, inconsistent translations it's no wonder that we've unknowingly thrown the baby out with the bath water when it comes to the Law.

It's The Law

Remember the "Torah" is translated as "Law" in the Greek when the more accurate translation in Hebrew is "instruction." So if Yahshua is the Word (Torah) made flesh, if He wrote the Torah with His finger, if He kept the Torah, and told us to walk as He walked, then we need to obey what He told us to do. "The one who says he stays in Him ought himself also to walk, even as He [Yahshua] walked" (1 John 2:6).

Quite the opposite of bringing an end to the Law, Yahshua came to "make it perfect" to "fill it up with meaning." He did not come to destroy or put an end to His own Law!

To get the correct view of the word "law," it will be necessary to carefully study each passage where it is used. Otherwise, it will be easy to get off track and unknowingly serve the one who is _not_ the Rock of our salvation.

Think about the poor translation of the term "law" as the right side of a pendulum representing the Church (without Torah). In the middle of the pendulum is Yahshua giving the correct interpretation (Torah / Law / Instructions made flesh). Then imagine the left side of the pendulum representing Rabbinic Judaism's view of the Law (legalism personified).

Let Yahshua Rock Your World

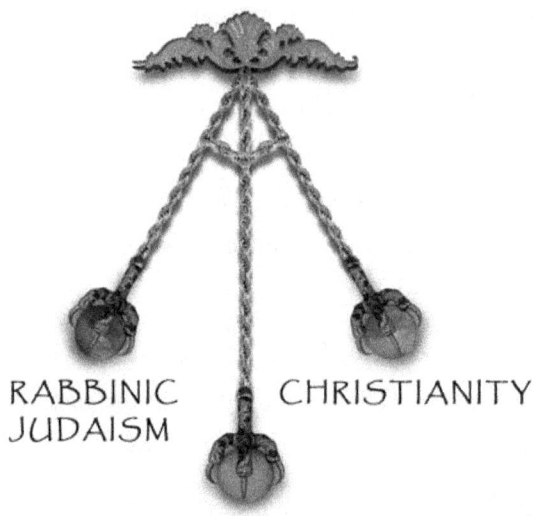

RABBINIC JUDAISM   CHRISTIANITY

TORAH/YAHSHUA

And it is the view of Rabbinic Judaism that we're going to touch on next. However, while it is not possible to cover this subject in depth in this short chapter, there are many resources available that go into great detail, one of which is Avi ben Mordechai's 500 page book titled "Galatians – A Torah-Based Commentary in First-Century Hebraic Context." With that said, let's take a peek at some of the legalisms introduced by the Pharisees…many of which are still observed today.

The four basic categories of the "oral law" are: (Halachot), (Takanot / Gezerah), (Ma'asim), and (Minhagim). We'll briefly define each one and give some examples.

Halachot – "to go" or "to walk." It refers to one's lifestyle. The Torah commands us to walk in a certain way. "The one who says he stays in Him ought himself also to walk, even as He [Yahshua] walked." (1 John 2:6). But the Pharisees and even many Rabbis today have established their own halachot – based on their private interpretation of Scripture – a twisted interpretation of the written Torah where context is irrelevant. On the other side of the pendulum, throughout Church history, Christian theologians have done plenty of twisting as well.

An example of Pharisaic *halacha*: The Scripture commands us not to do any ordinary work on the Sabbath. The Rabbis added 39 different categories and additional subcategories for what constitutes "work." One such enactment is: You're not allowed to flip a light switch because you're connecting a circuit (work), but you can use a timer on the Sabbath.

Another practice was to remove parts of the text and just leave a phrase that can be interpreted as a halacha favorable to their authority and control. This following example is actually one of their twisted halacha:

> "~~Do not~~ **follow a crowd** ~~to do evil, nor bear witness in a strife so as to turn aside after many, to turn aside what is right~~" (Exodus 23:2).

They use this phrase *(follow a crowd)* to instruct men to do what the majority of the Rabbis agree on without any regard for the context or what the actual text records. They just strike out what they consider irrelevant.

Takanot* and *Gezerah – "enactments and decrees of Pharisaic law." They are the commandments of the Rabbis. On the premise of "guarding" the Torah, they enacted additional laws as a way of putting a fence around the Torah, when actually these extra laws were used to enforce the authority of the Pharisees and later the Rabbis. Yahshua rebuked the Pharisees for their takanot. "…nullifying the Word of Elohim through your tradition [takanot] which you have handed down. And many such traditions you do" (Mark 7:13).

An example is their law requiring a daily ritual washing of hands which has nothing to do with hands that are dirty. This law teaches that when a person touches a holy book the hands become ritually impure. In other words, touching the Torah transmits uncleanness and washing their hands makes them pure again.

There is a law against "carrying" on Shabbat and that's why the Pharisees became unglued when Yahshua healed the man in John 5:8-10 and told him to pick up his bed and walk.

A final example in this category is a decree against handling and touching things prohibited for use on Shabbat and Holy days. This law included things like not having matches out on a table for fear that you might pick it up and light it. You're not allowed to carry a pen or a pencil in your pocket for fear that you might write with it on Shabbat.

This gives us an idea of what Paul was talking about in Colossians 2:20-21, "If, then, you died with Messiah from the elementary matters of the world, why, as though living in the world, do you subject yourselves to regulations: Do not touch, do not taste, do not handle." He was referring to the "oral law" of the

Pharisees. This was in no way an indictment of the true Torah which exists in Genesis and still exists in Revelation.

In Matthew 15, the Pharisees and scribes asked Yahshua why His disciples break the tradition of the elders. He answered by asking them why they break the Commandments of Elohim for the sake of their tradition. And in verses 8 and 9 He quoted Isaiah 29:13, "Wherefore the Lord [Yahweh] said, Forasmuch as this people draw near Me with their mouth, and with their lips do honour Me, but have removed their heart far from Me, and their fear toward Me is taught by the precept of men…" (KJV). So it was the commandments of men not the Commandments of Elohim that was the reason He confronted them.

Ma'asim is the next category – "work, do." It can reference work done by Elohim or by man. However, the Pharisees tweaked it to mean a law created for all Israel based on the repeated actions of a Pharisee. So if a devout Pharisee consistently performs an action, it sets a precedent and becomes law for all Israel. Biblical proof is not needed because in their thinking, Pharisaic authority supersedes Scriptural authority. Paul referred to these man-made laws as "works of the law."

Now Galatians 3:10 becomes clearer. When Paul wrote that **"For as many as are of the works of the Law are under the curse"** he was speaking about the oral tradition based upon the repetitive actions or deeds of a Pharisee. Therefore, those placing their confidence for salvation in the works of man are "under a curse" because they are rejecting the righteousness which Elohim has revealed in His Commandments (ALL TEN OF THEM). Also in Galatians 2:16 when Paul wrote, "**...a man is not justified by the works of the Law**" he was referring to the Pharisaic man-made commandments, not the Torah / Law of Elohim.

This is a vivid example of *ma'asim* Rabbinic style: There is a rule (work of the law) forbidding one to turn on a light switch on Shabbat because a famous Rabbi who lived from 1838 - 1933 did not turn on a light switch on Shabbat so it must be what the "oral law" requires.

Are you starting to get a picture of why Yahshua and Paul had such frequent confrontations with the Pharisees and those who followed their pattern of law?

Minhagim is our last category of Pharisaic law – These are legal traditions "customs" that are taught as Torah. The Rabbinic idea (Minhagim) is custom in Israel and is considered to be Torah.

For example your head must be covered if you are making a blessing or if you walk four cubits (roughly six feet). It's the custom – everyone is doing it, even though it's not the command of Elohim.

If a male was circumcised and it was not according to Pharisaic custom, he would have to be re-circumcised.

Sabbath restrictions under the category of minhagim are numerous (in the hundreds) but the following short list should make it easy to understand how the "sand / rock" of oral tradition is burdensome and is not at all what Yahweh had in mind for His people.

It's The Law

1. You cannot travel more than 2,000 cubits (roughly 3,000 feet) outside the city limits
2. One could not trim their fingernails
3. A man could not trim his beard or mustache
4. A woman could not put on makeup
5. One could not climb a tree, ride a beast, swim in water, clap their hands, slap their thighs (to music) or stamp their feet (to dancing)
6. If a man found two parchment boxes in the field, he was required to take them back to his house one at a time. If that man exceeded his travel limit he would have to hand it to a man who had not exceeded his limit
7. There were limits on how far a scroll could unroll before one was no longer permitted to roll it back up
8. Creeping things found in the temple could not be removed on the Sabbath
9. One could not draw water on the Sabbath while traveling or eat food unless it was prepared before the Sabbath
10. One could not help his beast give birth, or help it out if it fell into a well

This is nothing more than Rabbinic "bondage." What a burden! But obedience to Elohim's Torah leads to relationship, knowledge and blessing – it's a delight (read all of Psalm 119). So is there any wonder why the anti-Messiah wants us NOT to obey Torah. After all, disobedience to Elohim's Laws is obedience to *you know who*.

A resounding theme that's preached consistently in churches across America is "the Law was nailed to the tree when Yahshua was crucified – He brought an end to it." This is where it helps to know something about the culture. During Yahshua's time when a criminal was executed on a stake, it was common practice to nail a list of his crimes on the stake and THAT IS WHAT HE NAILED TO THE CROSS – the certificate of debt against us – the record of all our sins – NOT the Torah!

Paul became observant to the true Torah after his Damascus experience. His letters were mostly to correct those who were imposing oral traditions, to answer questions from new converts, and to encourage believers to remain faithful to the truth.

If Paul who was steeped in Pharisaic oral tradition – taught by the most learned Rabbi for most of his adult life – can come out of the false doctrines of the Pharisaic system so can we come out of the false Western, Greko / Roman system where we've inherited lies from our "church fathers."

Let's graft into the True Vine and leave man-made lies behind! "…let Elohim be True, and every man a liar…" (Romans 3:4).

I know these may be hard things to read especially for pastors and teachers, but don't take my word for it – search these things out for yourself. And just in case you think I am forgetting about "grace" I'm not, but I thought it was necessary to clear up some things about the Law. There is a lot of grace in the Old Covenant…even more than is in the New Covenant. Some of the words used in the New Covenant for grace have a different meaning than "grace." That may sound confusing, but what I am trying to say is the translator would use the word (grace) when a completely different word should have been used.

To learn more about this, I encourage you to use a Strong's Concordance and when you come across the word "grace" in the New Covenant, look it up and you will learn the correct word that should be used. How did this happen? Could it be as some believe that the translator had an agenda to prove there is more grace after the cross than before the cross? I have included some valuable information on grace in *Appendix 6*.

"If any of you lacks wisdom, let him ask of Elohim, who gives to all generously and without reproach..."
(James 1:5)

> "...Because I called, but no one answered. I spoke and they did not hear, and they did evil before My eyes, and chose what was displeasing to Me."
> *(Isaiah 66:4)*

Chapter 6: Idols, Idols Everywhere!

"You have no other mighty ones against My face."
(Exodus 20:3)

[You shall put no other gods against My face.]

"Oh you better watch out, you better not cry, you better not pout, I'm telling you why, Santa Clause is coming to town. He knows when you are sleeping. He knows when you're awake. He knows if you've been bad or good so be good for goodness sake." *Doesn't that sound like omnipotent, omnipresent talk?*

Thinking back, my world was *rocked* when I discovered toys in the closet just before Christmas – that's when Santa Claus became a myth to me. As a young child I was disappointed, but receiving gifts was still pretty cool. However, many children have been totally devastated upon finding out that Santa was not real and that their parents had lied to them.

Let Yahshua Rock Your World

Through deceit, the enemy has caused millions upon millions to fall into this lying trap!

You may think it's a harmless gesture to take your children to a shopping mall and sit them on Santa's lap; leave cookies and milk for Santa near the hearth; decorate a tree with silver and gold; hang wreaths and mistletoe, and give gifts under the pretense of celebrating the Messiah's birth. However, we're going to uncover some ROCKS of truth about the origin of this and other *un-holy* holidays celebrated by Christians everywhere.

In case you're about to have a nervous breakdown because I called Christmas an "unholy" holiday, just hang in there and we will get to the bottom of its origins. Digging deeper, we'll discover that it's a man-made season with customs that are pagan to the core – a holiday that displeases our Messiah.

Christmas has been described as the "season for giving." And indeed a spirit of gift giving seems to descend upon secular and religious people alike. It is so pervasive that Christian bookstores abound with items that remind us to "remember the reason for the season." We're going to discover that the *"reason"* we've all been taught is just a religious transparency overlaying pagan customs.

By the length to which some people go (way over budget), it seems as if there's an unspoken commandment to buy and exchange gifts. And in recent years, a special "must have" toy has been introduced and promoted as THE TOY that children everywhere simply must have – remember the Elmo craze a few years ago. Somehow the child that didn't get one was lacking in

Idols, Idols Everywhere

love – or something. What a great way for the enemy to teach our children from a very young age how *to covet* by "keeping up with the Joneses." It's like consumers on steroids! And you could literally get injured trying to beat the crowds for the latest craze before supplies run out.

In this hour, Yahweh is calling us back to His original seasons (Mo'edim) because there's not a lot of time left and He wants us to know His plan of redemption and to be "watching" for His return; both of which are tied to His Festivals. Yahweh's seasons (His Holy Convocations) have been clearly outlined in His instruction manual, the **Torah**. It is His *"plum line."*

Let me tell you from personal experience if you try to wallpaper a room without using a plum line, you'll find out how important one is. Without it, you're likely to have a real problem on your hands. Nothing is going to line up right because even though it may look straight, the only way you can tell for sure is to use a plum line. The same is true of His Torah. Without the solid ROCK of His instructions, we can easily end up thinking we're honoring Him when we're doing just the opposite *(remember the golden calf in Exodus? For more about this, see page 108).*

Getting back to Christmas, a lot of people find it to be the most depressing time of the year and statistics show that suicide rates usually go up during this season. Undoubtedly, STRESS is a major factor.

Okay what do we have so far? We have parents lying to their children, people expected to give gifts to one another, and others becoming depressed or suicidal more than any other time of the year. We need His plum line!

If we don't use His instruction manual, the Torah, as our plum line to make sure we stay on the straight and narrow path we can easily fall into the pit of celebrating *"unholy"* holidays. Ask yourself what the word Christmas, an evergreen tree, decorations galore, wreaths, holly berries, Yule logs, mistletoe, and December 25th have to do with our Savior? Not one thing!

Let's start with the word Christmas. It comes from two words: **1)** Christos (Greek) for anointed; and **2)** missa (Latin) meaning depart; and it was the last word spoken at a Catholic Mass. So the word Christmas means 'anointed-depart' *(interesting concept)*. First century believers knew nothing of this holiday. They celebrated Sukkot, the Feast of Tabernacles.

So where did this holiday and its customs get started?

The Ancient Babylonians celebrated the feast of the Son of Isis (goddess of nature) on December 25th.

> *Traditions*: Raucous partying, gluttonous eating and drinking, and gift-giving.

The ancient Greeks celebrated Bacchanalia to honor their god Dionysus, also called Bacchus, (the god of wine); it spread from Greece to Rome.

> *Traditions*: Singing, dancing and nocturnal orgies.

Idols, Idols Everywhere

The Romans celebrated Saturnalia honoring Saturn (the god of agriculture) during the Winter Solstice (meaning sun-stop), many years before Messiah. The Winter Solstice represents the shortest day of the year, i.e., between the sun rising and the sun setting which happens between December 22nd and December 25th. To Pagans, this meant that winter had ended and spring was coming. And they had a festival to celebrate it where they worshipped the sun for winning over the darkness of winter. This whole season was called Dies Natalis Invicti Solis, the Birthday of the Unconquered Sun.

> *Traditions*: Merrymaking; singers and dancers (called the Mummers) dressed in costumes and traveled from house to house entertaining their neighbors; [Christmas caroling was born from this custom]; businesses were closed except those that provided food or revelry; gambling, drinking, and feasting were encouraged; people exchanged gifts (called strenae), from the vegetation goddess Strenia; men dressed as women or in the hides of animals and caroused in the streets; and candles and lamps were used to frighten the spirits of darkness. The Romans also dated the winter solstice as December 25th.
>
> Regarding gift giving: At one time, human sacrifices were offered to Saturn; later, presents took the form of wax tapers and dolls during the Saturnalia. As we exchange Christmas presents, are

we unknowingly preserving (although under a different form) a most barbaric, savage custom?

In northern Europe, The pagans celebrated their own winter solstice, known as Yule; honoring Mithras (the sun god). It was also known as the Twelve Nights – celebrated from December 25th to January 6th.

Traditions: It was customary to light a candle to encourage Mithras, and the sun, to reappear next year. Huge **Yule logs** were burned in honor of the sun. **Mistletoe** was considered a sacred plant, and the custom of kissing under the mistletoe began as a fertility ritual. **Hollyberries** were thought to be a food of the gods. Live **evergreen trees** were often brought into homes. Shrines and other sacred places were decorated with **holly**, **ivy**, and **bay**. It was a time for feasting and drinking.

When Christmas was introduced in the fourth century, converts were told to worship the *Son of God* instead of the *sun god*. Although the focus of the holiday changed, the pagan customs and practices remained mostly unchanged; they were just given **invented** Christian meanings. Ecclesiastes 7:29 proclaims, "Lo, this only have I found, that God [Elohim] hath made man upright; but they have sought out many *inventions*" (KJV).

Are you starting to see that this holiday is nothing more than an invented copy of a pagan observance?

Idols, Idols Everywhere

Again, first century believers never observed Christmas; they celebrated the customary "Feasts of Yahweh" that are listed in Leviticus 23. In fact, Christmas was not celebrated in Rome until about 300 years after Messiah's death. In an effort to convert the Roman pagans to Christianity, Pope Julius I declared that Messiah's birth would be celebrated on December 25th the date that corresponded to the pagan's feast. This was a major departure from those exhorted to "earnestly contend for the belief which was once for all delivered to the Set-Apart ones" (see Jude 3).

You may be thinking, *"even if Christmas does have pagan origins it doesn't mean that to me."* Many even say that all its customs have been Christianized so it's now acceptable to Yahweh. Well, exactly who Christianized it? MEN! Did they get the Father's permission? NO! Regardless of our good intentions, He's the One who decides how we are to love and honor Him.

> **"Here is what Yahweh says, 'Don't learn the way of the heathen…for the customs of the peoples are nothing. They cut down a tree in the forest; a craftsman works it with his axe; they deck it with silver and gold. They fix it with hammer and nails, so that it won't move' " (Jeremiah 10:2-4).**

> **"You shall not worship Yahweh your Elohim in that way, for every abominable thing that Yahweh hates they have done for their gods…" (Deuteronomy 12:31).**

Let Yahshua Rock Your World

When we find out that He hates these things, shouldn't we change and repent – no matter how difficult it seems to our flesh. Speaking of our flesh, it will always be offended by His Word because it does not want to obey. But if we desire to please Him, we can't continually walk in the flesh because He's looking for those who will worship Him in Spirit and in Truth. We've been deceived for centuries into thinking we're pleasing Him when in fact we're "displeasing" Him when we celebrate pagan holidays. *(Even if we have "good" intentions – golden calves are still golden calves.)*

So far, we've discussed many of the customs associated with pre-Christian pagan celebrations on or around December 25th and their undeniable similarity to Christmas customs. Now it's time for a closer look at what Scripture reveals about the time of the Messiah's birth that would make December 25th extremely improbable as the correct date.

First of all Luke 2:7-8 reveals that shepherds were in the fields watching their flocks at the time of His birth. However, shepherds would not be spending the night in the fields guarding their flocks during December because it is cold and rainy in Judea. Further, there would not be any pasturage at that time.

Second, according to Luke 2:1-4, Yahshua's parents came to Bethlehem to register in the census ordered by Caesar Augustus. Taking a census when temperatures often dropped below freezing and roads were in poor condition would have been self-defeating. Therefore, such censuses were not taken in winter.

Idols, Idols Everywhere

Third, it would have been nearly impossible for His mother, Miryam (Mary), to make such a journey of about 70 miles through a hill district averaging about 3,000 feet above sea-level, in the dead of winter.

Finally, history reveals that Yahshua's birth most likely took place in the fall during the first day of the *Feast of Tabernacles* making crystal clear the meaning of John 1:14, "And the Word *became flesh* and pitched His *tent* [Tabernacled] among us..." This Feast is seven days long and the next day, the **eighth day** (when Messiah would have been circumcised), is a high Sabbath known as the Last Great Day.

According to Biblical accounts, Elisheva (Elizabeth) was six months pregnant when Miriam (Mary) conceived Yahshua (see Luke 1:24-36). So if we can determine Yochanan's (John's) conception and birth, we can determine the approximate time of year Yahshua was born. Priests served in the Temple during specific "courses" throughout the year and Z'kharyah (Zacharias), served during the course of Abiyah (Luke 1:5). Historical calculations indicate this course of service corresponded to June 13-19 in that year. You can view the details from the following link: *http://levendwater.org/companion/append179.html#times.*

It was during this time period, in verses 8 – 13, that Z'kharyah learned that his wife, Elisheva, would bear him a son. Counting six months forward from June, we come to December, the month that Yahshua would have been CONCEIVED. Counting nine months forward from December, we reach the month of September – the month He would have been BORN. Obviously, He wasn't born on some pagan holiday as we've been led to believe for the last 2,000 years.

Let's review again: We have parents lying to their children, shopping gone wild, depression and suicidal tendencies on the rise, pagan customs, and the wrong date of His birth. Think about it, can He really be pleased just because we think in our minds that we're honoring Him? He says, "This people draw near to Me with their mouth, and respect Me with their lips, but their heart is far from Me. But in vain do they worship Me..." (Matthew 15:8-9a). Whether we're willing to admit it or not Christianity has its own *"golden calves."*

Again, we're much too close to the end to continue playing around with pagan rocks. So let's get back to the "ROCK" of our salvation and leave those unholy rocks behind. The mixture of a pagan holiday with a religious overlay is not pleasing in His sight. When we celebrate Christmas, we are literally putting other gods in His face, whether we think we are or not. It really isn't any different than what the children of Israel did at Mount Sinai. Did they not say *after they fashioned the golden calf,* "Tomorrow is a festival to Yahweh" (Exodus 32:5)? They were worshipping Him in a pagan manner. He didn't like it then and He doesn't like it now!

From Genesis to Revelation Yahweh instructs us to be Set-Apart (Holy). He absolutely will not share His Glory with another. His Ways are higher than our ways and the only way we can know how to please Him is to study His Word *and* follow His Instructions.

Idols, Idols Everywhere

Here's a formula for you:

Pagan roots + shopping blitz + Satan's birthday = a recipe for destruction!

This next ROCK of revelation sent shock waves down my spine. Yes, I'm talking about another cherished *"un-holy"* Christian holiday. EASTER! Just like Christmas, Easter was not considered a "Christian" holiday until the fourth century. The first century believers celebrated Passover according to Leviticus 23:5.

There was always a lot of excitement in our home surrounding Easter. As kids growing up, my sisters and I knew for sure that we would get new outfits (from head to toe) for Easter. Frilly dresses and socks, new white Patten leathered shoes, dressy purses, and bonnets with ribbon hanging down the back, was the usual fare.

We really made dying Easter eggs a true art. I'll never forget when the paper patterns came out that allowed you to make some very impressive designs on your eggs. We so looked forward to coloring our eggs; but the hunt…that was the ultimate goal. Trees, flower pots, shrubs, and outdoor furniture were all likely candidates of concealment. On rainy days, we'd just hide eggs inside our house. But if you wanted lots of variety, the Church Easter egg hunt was the best.

Year after year, like most families, we celebrated Easter without knowing of its pagan trappings. However, as a young adult, I began to wonder about why people wore new clothes; gave their kids Easter baskets; chocolate rabbits; dyed eggs, and served ham for dinner on Easter Sun-day. And I never imagined that by attending Easter sunrise services, I was participating in the same ancient pagan ritual that is still practiced in England today.

I thought I was celebrating the resurrection of Messiah…that's what I thought because that's what I'd been taught. However, history has revealed some obvious truths about this holiday that ROCKED my understanding and showed me that I was worshipping some camouflaged ancient pagan idol. Keep in mind the chapter titled "If I Were The Enemy" and how stealth the enemy is at destroying Yahweh's people. In John 10:10 Yahshua warned us that, "The thief does not come except to steal, and to slaughter, and to destroy." And we find another destructive pagan custom below:

> Typical Christian sunrise services are held outside where participants face the east so they can see the sun come up during the service. In Ezekiel 8:15-16 Yahweh spoke to Ezekiel: "Then He (Yahweh) said to me (Ezekiel), 'Have you seen this, O son of man? You are to see still greater abominations than these.' And He brought me into the inner court of the House of Yahweh. And there, at the door of the Hĕkal (Temple) of Yahweh, between the porch and the altar, were about twenty-five men with their backs toward the Hĕkal (Temple) of Yahweh and their faces toward the east, and they were bowing themselves eastward to the sun." *(There is nothing new under the sun, Ecclesiastes 1:9.)*

Idols, Idols Everywhere

Yahweh is not pleased when we do the same things idolaters do. He wants us to love Him the way **He wants** not the way **we want**. How do we show that we love Him? He gives us the answer in His Word.

> **Exodus 20:6**, "…and showing mercy unto thousands of them that love Me and keep My Commandments" (KJV).
>
> **John 14:15**, "If you love Me, you shall guard [keep / do] My Commands."
>
> **John 14:21**, "He who possesses My Commands and guards [keeps / does] them, it is he who loves Me. And he who loves Me shall be loved by My Father, and I shall love him and manifest Myself to him."
>
> **John 15:14**, "You are My friends if you do whatever I Command you."
>
> **1 John 5:3**, "For this is the love for Elohim, that we guard [keep / do] His Commands…"
>
> **2 John 1:6**, "And this is the love, that we walk [do] according to His Commands."
>
> **Deuteronomy 7:9**, "And you shall know that Yahweh your Elohim, He is Elohim, the trustworthy Ěl guarding [keeping / doing] Covenant and kindness for a thousand generations with those who love Him, and those who guard [keep / do] His Commands…"

From these verses we see that keeping Yahweh's Commandments are important, and Easter is not one of them, but the enemy has put this pagan celebration right against His face, without even changing its pagan *name* or its *customs*. When Yahshua talks about keeping His Commandments, He's referring to the Ten Commandments found in the Tanakh (Old Covenant), because the New Covenant did not exist at this time.

In order to justify calling Easter a Christian holiday, the enemy had to sneak it into one Bible translation, at least one time (see Acts 12:4 KJV). However, The Companion Bible's margin notes for Acts 12:4 on page 1607 reads, "Easter is a heathen term, derived from the Saxon goddess *Eastre*, the same as Astarte, the Syrian Venus, called Ashtoreth in the O.T." The margin notes also reflect that "Easter" in that passage is actually the Greek word *pascha* or Passover. It's a **mistranslation** in the King James Version! Although some would like us to believe that Easter is just another name for Passover, in reality there are no similarities, as you will see later.

So why do you suppose the translators chose to use the name of a heathen goddess – also known as the "Queen of Heaven" – instead of the correct translation used elsewhere in the New Covenant? Could it be anti-Semitism residing in the hearts of the translators, fueled by Satan that caused this and other errors in the New Covenant? *(Google: errors in the King James Version and you'll find plenty.)* This particular error has been corrected in other translations, even in the NKJV. However, it seems the damage has

Idols, Idols Everywhere

already been done because the whole world thinks that Easter is actually a Christian holiday sanctioned by Elohim, when it is not.

Just as we did in the section regarding the customs of Christmas, we should ask ourselves what hot cross buns, died eggs, bunnies, bonnets, and lilies have to do with our Messiah's resurrection? NOT ONE THING! Yet it's observed on the same day that all the sun-worshippers celebrated Easter / Eastre / Astarte / Ashtoreth (using these same customs) for thousands of years.

In his book "Fossilized Customs," Lew White writes, "Easter was already one of the two biggest celebrations observed by Pagans, long before Christianity came along. The festival involved the *"Rights of Spring"* near the Equinox of Venus, when Pagans believed the Earth Mother was **impregnated by the sun**. They engaged in ritual sex acts, and used symbols of fertility like eggs, rabbits and hot cross buns. Her emblem was the flower of the lily." Alexander Hislop cites in his book "The Two Babylons," that hot cross buns were used in the worship of Cecrops, the founder of Athens, 1500 years before the Christian era. That being true, how did these customs become part of our Christian heritage?

We have Constantine to thank for merging paganism with Christianity by **inventing** "so called" Christian holidays on pagan days, using pagan customs. It's called syncretism. And as I mentioned before, the early assembly of believers kept Passover. They did so for nearly 300 years until it was outlawed by Constantine in about 325 A.D.

His proclamations were forcefully carried out. For example, anyone caught celebrating Easter on any day other than the first Sunday after the spring equinox would be excommunicated, severely punished, or ***even killed.***

I had a real wake-up call when I discovered these truths and realized that just because everybody is celebrating Christmas and Easter doesn't make it right in the eyes of Yahweh. He has commanded us to keep His Festivals, which give details about His first coming and His second coming. But we have kicked out the True ROCK and fallen for a "counterfeit."

Here's an example of just how pervasive the *counterfeit* is: In the concordance section of my copy of the King James Version, the word **Passover is missing**, although there are at least *eleven* references to it in the New Covenant alone, not to mention the number of times it's mentioned in the Old Covenant. However, the word **Easter is included** although there is only *one* reference to it, and that reference is a blatant <u>mistranslation</u>. Humm! Yes, there is a conspiracy and it has been going on for centuries. The enemy knows "it only takes a little leaven to leaven the whole lump." In the Scriptures, we are commanded to keep Passover, but a commandment to observe Easter cannot be found.

One of the ways the enemy has been masterfully deceptive is by convincing Christians that the Feasts found in the Tanakh (Old Covenant) are the Yahudim (Jews) feasts. But a careful reading of Leviticus 23:2 clearly shows that they are Yahweh's Feasts.

Idols, Idols Everywhere

"Speak to the children of Yisra'ĕl (Israel), and say to them, 'The **Appointed Times of Yahweh**, which you are to proclaim as Set-Apart gatherings, **My Appointed Times, are these**.'"

Not only are they Yahweh's Feasts, but they are for the stranger as well the home born.

"There is **one Torah for the native-born and for the stranger** who sojourns among you" (Exodus 12:49).

"And when a stranger sojourns among you, then he shall perform the Passover of Yahweh. He shall do so according to the Law [Torah / Instructions] of the Passover and according to its right-ruling. **You have one Law** [Torah / Instruction], **both for the stranger and the native of the land**" (Numbers 9:14).

"One Law [Torah / Instruction] is for you [the Israelite] of the assembly and for the stranger [non-Israelite] who sojourns with you – a Law [Torah / Instruction] forever throughout your generations. **As you are, so is the stranger before Yahweh.** One Torah and one right-ruling is for you [the Israelite] and for the stranger [non-Israelite] who sojourns with you" (Numbers 15:15-16).

When we receive Yahshua as Savior, Romans 11 teaches that we (Gentiles) are grafted in among the home born and have become equal sharers in the rich root of the olive tree (Yahshua), and we shouldn't boast as if we were better than the branches

(Israel)! We become members of the commonwealth of Israel. And there is much we can learn from the branches…not the Pharisaic legalisms of the oral torah…but the True Torah.

From the very beginning Satan has been scheming to get people to transgress Elohim's Laws…it started in the Garden of Eden. And non-biblical practices are some of his chief devices. If Yahweh didn't accept pagan festivals back then, does He accept them now as a part of our worship to Him, even if they've been "so called" *Christianized*? NO!

No matter how independent we may feel we have to remember that we are dependent upon Him. He made us; we didn't make ourselves; we are the sheep of His pasture and guess what? He has His own Festivals which are His *Appointed Times* that He wants to meet with us for our wedding rehearsals. But for the most part, the Church has said, "No thank you."

There are many resources (books and websites) that go into great detail about the Biblical Feast days. Some are listed in the resource section at the end of this book. However, included below is a brief overview of Yahweh's Passover and seven annual Sabbaths, with an explanation of their prophetic significance (excerpts have been taken from Lew White's book *The Torah Zone*).

First, we'll briefly explore the Passover which is not a Sabbath but a memorial to remember Messiah's death; then we'll move on to the seven annual Sabbaths. Every one of them points to Messiah – what He has already fulfilled or what He has yet to fulfill.

Idols, Idols Everywhere

PASSOVER

Foreshadowing the redemption of all mankind, the blood of the first lamb, slain in the Garden of Eden, was shed to cover our original parents, Adam and Chavvah (Eve). Then Yahshua the Redeemer delivered Israel out of the land of Egypt with an "outstretched arm." The sacrificial blood marked the "door" in a special way (on the lintel and two door posts), to show how He covers and atones for us. Yahweh has provided HIMSELF as a Lamb, *who takes away the sins of the world*. Now we are marked as belonging to Him when we receive Him through grace by faith and keep His Commandments. Our decision to obey is marked by our observance of this shadow of things to come. (**There is going to be a second Exodus!**)

The Biblical year begins with Pesach (Passover), in the spring rather than winter. This Feast falls in the month of March / April. During this time, we remember the protection and deliverance of all Israel (including the mixed multitude) as they were rescued from their bondage in Egypt. The blood on the doorposts signifies the wounds He bore for us and that He told us to remember Him and *His death* by the emblems of bread and wine as we observe each Passover. In John 15:13 we see that His death shows His great love for us.

UNLEAVENED BREAD

Now that our sins have been atoned for [Passover] and we've accepted that atonement, let's move on to the Feast of Unleavened Bread. This Feast falls in the same month as Passover. (Hag HaMatsch is the Hebrew word for unleavened bread.) Leaven in the Scripture represents sin. This is the time that we get those false rocks, boulders, and weeds of "sin" out of the soil of our hearts by repenting. Removing leaven and keeping it out of our homes for seven days is a shadow of preparing the soil to receive the SEED.

The 1st Day of Hag HaMatsch [*1st annual High Sabbath*] is a day of rest recalling Israel's departure from Egypt – Satan's kingdom. Israel's departure (repentance) from Satan's rule is the keynote of this day.

The 7th Day of Hag HaMatsch [*2nd annual High Sabbath*] corresponds to Israel crossing the "red sea" on dry ground. It also relates to the flood when Noah's family went into the waters and represents our covenant immersion act (death to sin). Repentance is the first step away from sin and immersion is the second step.

During this seven day period the "**wave sheaf offering,**" is observed in remembrance of the resurrection of Yahshua, our High Priest who died as our Passover Lamb but then raised to immortality. This foreshadows the redemption of our bodies. Since the **Bikkurim (First Fruits)** have been waved (Yahshua's resurrection, 1 Corinthians 15:20), we look forward with anticipation to the forthcoming harvest. Again, First Fruits falls in the same month as Passover.

SHAVUOTH / PENTECOST

Shavuoth [*3rd annual High Sabbath*] also known as Pentecost in the Christian Church, foreshadows Messiah's Circumcision of our heart, where He removes the heart of stone and replaces it with a heart of flesh, so we can love His Truth, the TORAH. The Feast of Pentecost falls fifty days from First Fruits. Usually this happens between April / May. After clearing the ground during the seven day Feast of Unleavened Bread,

Idols, Idols Everywhere

we are planted with the Good Seed (His Torah) during Shavuoth. This is when the bride says, "I Do," to her husband "...All the Words which Yahweh has spoken we shall do" (Exodus 24:3).

During this time we remember our wedding vows, the Ten Commandments, first given at Mt. Sinai (then written in stone), but now written on our hearts by the Spirit. (See Jeremiah 31:31-34, Ezekiel 36:26, 27, and Hebrews Chapters 8 and 10.) The evidence that we are His is revealed when we practice obeying His Commandments.

FEAST OF TRUMPETS / YOM TERUAH

Trumpets [*4th annual High Sabbath*] observed at the beginning of the seventh biblical month is a final warning, a day for the blowing of the shofar foreshadowing the 'last trump' when Yahshua returns to earth to gather His elect from the four winds of the earth (Matthew 24:31). It is also mentioned in 1 Thessalonians 4:16. This Feast usually falls in August / September.

YOM KIPPUR / THE DAY OF ATONEMENT

Yom Kippur [*5th annual High Sabbath*] is observed on the 10th day of the 7th biblical month and is a very important Holy day. It's a day set aside to atone for the sins between man and Elohim during the past year. It is a complete fast day (Acts 27:9), and foreshadows the day when the Judge of all flesh will look at each person and decide whether or not they are of the "wheat" or "tares" and **separate them** as with a winnowing fork. This Feast usually falls in September / October.

FEAST OF TABERNACLES / SUKKOT / BOOTHS

Tabernacles [*6th annual High Sabbath*], is celebrated for 7 days and looking back, we remember the provisions Elohim made for us in the wilderness. Looking forward it points to the millennial rule of Yahshua on earth following His return. It is also called "the Feast of the Ingathering." It is a Feast spent learning what the Kingdom of Elohim will be like. At this annual Sabbath, we come out of the world and the temporary shelters we live in at Tabernacles teach us that we are only temporarily in this present world, which is not our true home. In our true home, Yahweh's righteous standards will be in full force and all people will be compliant. This Feast usually falls in September / October.

THE LAST GREAT DAY

The Eighth Day [*7th annual High Sabbath*], is also known as **Simchat Torah** which means rejoicing with Torah. At the end of the Feast of Tabernacles is a Sabbath (a Holy Convocation) representing the final Sabbath, the eternal one that Yahweh had intended from the very beginning. It foreshadows the post-millennial earth and a time when Yahweh will bring His own throne to the planet in the New Yerushalyim (Jerusalem), where Israel's redemption is completely fulfilled and we are clothed with immortality, and enter into the New Yerushalyim (1 Corinthians 15:24-28; Revelation 21). Halleluyah!

Are there New Covenant examples of people keeping or intending to keep the Feasts? Yes.

Idols, Idols Everywhere

Luke 2:42, "And when He (Yahshua) was twelve years old, they went up to Yerushalayim (Jerusalem) according to the practice of the Festival."

John 5:1, "After this there was a Festival of the Yahudim (Jews), and Yahshua went up to Yerushalayim (Jerusalem)."

John 12:20, "And there were certain Greeks among those coming up to worship at the Festival."

Matthew 26:2, "You know that after two days the Passover takes place, and the Son of Adam is to be delivered up to be impaled."

1 Corinthians 5:8, "So then let us observe the Festival, not with old leaven, nor with the leaven of evil and wickedness, but with the unleavened bread of sincerity and truth."

Acts 18:21, "...but took leave of them, saying, 'I have to keep this coming Festival in Yerushalayim (Jerusalem) by all means, but I shall come back to you, Elohim desiring so.' And he [Paul] sailed from Ephesos (Ephesus)."

Why are the Feasts still being observed in the New Covenant?

Yahweh declares the Feasts "a statute *forever*" (Exodus 12:14, 17, 24, 42; Leviticus 23:14, 21, 31, and 41).

Let Yahshua Rock Your World

Will believers keep the Feasts in Yahweh's coming Kingdom? Yes.

Isaiah 66:23, "And it shall be that from New Moon to New Moon, and from Sabbath to Sabbath, all flesh shall come to worship before Me, declares Yahweh."

Zechariah 14:16-19, "And it shall be that all who are left from all the gentiles which came up against Yerushalayim, shall go up from year to year to bow themselves to the Sovereign, Yahweh of hosts, and to observe the Festival of Booths [Tabernacles]. And it shall be, that if anyone of the clans of the earth does not come up to Yerushalayim to bow himself to the Sovereign, Yahweh of hosts, on them there is to be no rain. And if the clan of Mitsrayim [Egypt] does not come up and enter in, then there is no rain. On them is the plague with which Yahweh plagues the gentiles who do not come up to observe the Festival of Booths [Tabernacles]. This is the punishment of Mitsrayim [Egypt] and the punishment of all the gentiles that do not come up to observe the Festival of Booths [Tabernacles]."

Ezekiel 44:24, "…And they are to guard My Torot [Laws] and My laws [Statutes] in all My Appointed Festivals, and Set Apart My Sabbaths."

Idols, Idols Everywhere

Ezekiel 45:21, "In the first [biblical] month, on the fourteenth day of the month, you have the Passover, a Festival of seven days, unleavened bread is eaten."

Ezekiel 46:3, "And the people of the land shall also bow themselves at the entrance to this gate before Yahweh, on the Sabbaths and on the New Moons."

Matthew 26:29; Mark 14:25; Luke 22:18, 30, Yahshua Himself promised to keep the Passover in the future Kingdom with His disciples.

As you can see, not only were the Feast days kept in the Old and New Covenant, but everyone, including Yahshua, will keep them when His Kingdom comes to earth.

The enemy has been busy for centuries keeping us blind to these Truths, but Yahweh, our ROCK, always has the last Word.

"Do you not know that the unrighteous shall not inherit the reign of Elohim? Do not be deceived. Neither those who whore, nor **idolaters**, nor adulterers, nor effeminate, nor homosexuals, nor thieves, nor greedy of gain, nor drunkards, nor revilers, nor swindlers shall inherit the reign of Elohim."
(1 Corinthians 6:9-10)

Let Yahshua Rock Your World

> "Blessed are those doing His commands, so that the authority shall be theirs unto the tree of life, and to enter through the gates into the city."
> (Revelation 22:14

Conclusion

Chapter 7: Conclusion

> Let us hear the conclusion of the entire matter:
> Fear Elohim and **guard** [keep / do] **His Commands**,
> for this *applies* to all mankind!
> Ecclesiastes 12:13

If you're having trouble wrapping your brain around some of the truths in this book and you feel like you have "brain freeze," you are not alone. Many false doctrines have been set into our minds through "bed-rock" indoctrination (since the time of Constantine), that will require breaking up the fallow ground *first* before we can receive Yahweh's True Seed.

In this hour, the Father is exposing centuries-old lies and false doctrines, and He is drawing myriads all over the world back to their First Love, Himself, through His Truth. And just like the "Bereans," we should **receive the Word with eagerness of mind (an open mind) and search the Scriptures daily** as they did to see whether or not the teachings they heard were true. By the way, the Scripture they searched was the Tanakh (Old Covenant), because the B'rit Hadasha (Renewed / New Covenant) wasn't written yet.

Let Yahshua Rock Your World

As Rico Cortes (a popular Hebrew Roots teacher) would say, "Don't believe anything that I say but search out everything that I say for yourself." The Father is revealing much more than what is covered in this book. Therefore, I encourage you to do some research on your own. The Resource section in this book is a good place to start. It will take some time but it will be worth every minute.

Yahweh is getting His (remnant) people ready for His return, and He can use anyone or anything He wants even if it's a donkey (like the one that spoke to Balaam). So don't dismiss the contents of this book just because it comes from a source other than a person standing in a pulpit on Sun-day morning with a lot of degrees behind his or her name.

Most who read this book may have taken the first step of receiving and confessing Yahshua (Jesus) as Savior, but there is more to being **in Him** and **loving Him** than just saying the "sinner's prayer," "faithfully attending the *right* Church," "serving," "giving," and "believing." He's calling us to be **doers** of His Word. ***His Word is the Torah.***

The Christian message from our Western / Greco-Roman mindset is a GMO – a Genetically Modified Organism. It looks like Elohim (God), sounds like Elohim (God), but it's a mixed (lukewarm) message. We've been taught: The favor of God is expressed in material things; that we're no longer under the Law, but under grace. On the surface – and through mistranslations – there may "appear" to be Scriptures that support those beliefs

Conclusion

(especially when looking through a Western / Greko-Roman lens). But studying from a Hebraic perspective proves otherwise.

Actually, we've been taught to do exactly the opposite of what Yahweh commands. He tells us to keep **His Commandments** and we say, "They've been done away with." He tells us to keep **His Feast Days** and we say, "We'll honor You with our own holidays." He tells us to meet with Him on Saturday for **Shabbat** (the day He sanctified), and we tell Him to, "Meet with us on Sunday." He tells us His Name is **Yahweh** and His Son's Name is **Yahshua**, but we call Him by the titles God, Lord, and a Greek name, Jesus. He tells us what is **clean** and what is **unclean** and we tell Him, "We can eat whatever we want."

But when we delve deeper, wearing a Hebraic lens we find some fascinating truths. For instance:

- The New Covenant is not NEW; covenants are everlasting. The more accurate translation is "re-newed" or "refreshed" (see Strong's #2537).

- Yahshua is found throughout the Scriptures – He is the Word (Law / Torah / Instruction) in the beginning made flesh (John 1:1). He manifested as a ROCK at Horeb in Exodus 17:6; as a burning Bush in Exodus 3:2; as a Messenger to Abraham in Genesis 18:1; and to Joshua as Captain of the host of Yahweh in Joshua 5:14. He wrestled with Jacob in

Genesis 32:24-28; and nearly every time you read the word "Salvation" in the Old Covenant, it's referring to Yahshua.

- There is more grace in the Old Covenant than in the Renewed / New Covenant and the Old Covenant Law is referred to in more than 1,050 places in the Renewed / New Covenant as revealed by ***Dake's Annotated Reference Bible.***

- We find that the "Church" didn't start in the Book of Acts, it started at Mt. Sinai. The called-out assembly is *kahal* in Hebrew and *ekklesia* in Greek.

- The Sabbath began in Genesis 2:3 before there was a Hebrew, Jew, or Israelite.

- Adam, Cain, Able, Noah and others already knew what animals were "clean" and "unclean" before the Law was ever written down. Interestingly, the first commandment given to man was in reference to food (Genesis 2:16).

This truth ROCKED my world:

"And by this we know that **we know Him, if we guard** [keep/do] **His Commands. The one who says, "I know Him," and does not guard**

Conclusion

> [keep/do] **His Commands, is a liar**, and the truth is not in him. But **whoever guards His Word, truly the love of Elohim has been perfected in him.** By this we know that we are in Him. **The one who says he stays in Him ought himself also to walk, even as He walked**" (1 John 2:3-6).

According to the above Scripture, I was not IN HIM, I did not KNOW HIM, I was a LIAR, I did not LOVE HIM and I did not ABIDE IN HIM, because I was not keeping all ten of His Commandments, just some of them.

> "Whoever, then, breaks one of the least of these Commands, and teaches men so, shall be called least in the reign of the heavens; but whoever **does** and **teaches** them, he shall be called great in the reign of the heavens" (Matthew 5:19).

Studying the Scriptures from a Hebraic perspective revealed that I was ignorant of even a basic understanding of His Word although I'd studied it for many years. The dictionary describes the word "ignorant" as: **1)** lacking knowledge or experience, **2)** caused by or showing lack of knowledge, **3)** unaware. And because I was unaware of the Hebraic idioms, I did not have the knowledge I needed to rightly divide His Word. It reminds me of the movie "Cool Hand Luke," where the recurring theme throughout that movie was, "What we have here is a failure to communicate." When we apply a 21st century Western Greco-Roman understanding to the Word of Elohim instead of a Hebraic understanding, a communications problem occurs because it was written by Hebrews to Hebrews.

A perfect example is Deuteronomy 6:4 which starts out with the English word "Hear." The English dictionary defines "hear" as: **1)** to be aware of (sounds) by the ear, **2)** to listen to, **3)** to conduct a hearing of (a law case, etc.), **4)** to be informed of; to learn.

But in Hebrew the word for "hear" is "Sh'ma." It appears 1159 times in the Tanakh (Old Covenant) alone and it means not only to *"hear,"* but *"understand"* and *"obey"* as well. It's all about action. The root of "**sh'ma**" is "**ma**" and means "**intestines**." It speaks to internalizing the Word so that it becomes a part of us. Its Hebrew spelling is Shin-(ש) Mem-(מ) Ayin (ע). Shin (ש), among other things, means "El Shaddai" (El is Sufficient) and the "Eternal Flame" or "Divine Revelation." Mem (מ) is mayim which means "water;" also the "Word" or "Torah." Ayin (ע) is the "Fountain" or "Eye." So, in the word "sh'ma" we hear "El Shaddai's Revelation," the "Torah" which is like a "Fountain" (Living Water).

This is just one example out of thousands that show if we get the Hebrew context wrong, we're going to get Yahshua wrong.

The more we dig into the ROCK of our Hebrew Roots, the richer and deeper our understanding will be. For me, studying the Torah from a Hebraic perspective has been like trying to contain Niagara Falls. Isaiah 11:9b reads:

> "…for the earth shall be filled with the knowledge
> of Yahweh as the waters cover the sea."

Conclusion

As we start walking as Yahshua walked, we will find ourselves keeping His Commandments including His Sabbaths and His Feast days; we'll start using His Hebrew name and His Father's Hebrew name; and we will only eat what He approves as food. This is how He wants us to worship Him (in Spirit and in Truth).

The Sabbath deserves another mention here. Again, it's like having a vacation day each week with Elohim...it is a delight. It marks those who belong to Him. We stop our work and honor His work (creation). And, it will continue **FOREVER**! Isaiah 66:22-24 speaks of a future time when there is a new heaven and a new earth and we see that time is still reckoned from Sabbath to Sabbath. Also, Matthew 24:20 reflects a future time with the instruction to "...pray that your flight does not take place in winter **or on the Sabbath**." And Hebrews 4:1-11 clearly speaks of the future, "**So there remains a Sabbath-keeping** for the people of Elohim." (Some translations render it: "there remains a rest," but the literal translation is Sabbath-keeping.) When Yahshua referred to Himself as Yahweh of the Sabbath He was declaring that He is the One Who determines what is proper and improper to do on the Sabbath. He was not implying that He was doing away with it or changing it from Saturday to Sunday.

Like many of you, I have read Scripture verses referring to the Sabbath for years, but I didn't have a clue that it applied to anyone other than the Yahudim (Jews) because that's what I'd been taught. However, changing the seventh day Sabbath to the first day of the week Sunday is one of the dominant ways the enemy has caused the Church to "fall away" and considering this deception has been going on for centuries, it's not at all surprising that we find ourselves in this fallen state today.

When you look at history, you'll find that many of the doctrines in the modern Church came straight from Rome. In fact, nearly every Church in America could add the word "Catholic" to its name and be accurate, i.e., the First Baptist "Catholic" Church; Lutheran "Catholic" Church; Presbyterian "Catholic" Church; Church of Christ "Catholic" Church; New Covenant "Catholic" Church; St. Peter's Episcopal "Catholic" Church; or United Pentecostal "Catholic" Church. Why? Because although they may have reformed a few things, they **ALL** worship on Sunday, keep pagan holidays and don't observe Yahweh's Feast days or Dietary Laws.

Yahshua asked a very profound question in Luke 6:46, "**But why do you call Me 'Master, Master,' and do not do what I say?**" Instead of Him saying, "Well done, good and trustworthy servant." I'm afraid that many will hear Him say; "I never knew you" because we have not obeyed His Commands but have followed the traditions of men.

Can we really love one another without loving Elohim and keeping His Commandments?

> "By this we know that we love the children of Elohim, **when we love Elohim and guard** [keep / do] **His Commands**. For this is the love for Elohim, that we guard [keep / do] His Commands, and His Commands are not heavy…" (1 John 5:2-3).

Conclusion

I realize that when you start to embrace these Truths there will be tremendous pressure not to "rock" the boat, but it's better for the boat to be "rocked" by the revelation of Yahshua than to be blown "to" and "fro" by every wind of doctrine (see Ephesians 4:14).

Have you ever wondered why the Church has so little influence on the culture? I am convinced that it's because the enemy has crept in and stealthily weaved a hybrid causing the Church to produce mixed fruit instead of Yahweh's kind of (Torah observant) fruit. There is sin in the camp! And we have covered it up with "grace." But when we continue in "sin" (lawlessness / Torahlessness), that's a dis-grace because we are dis-ing the grace that we have been given and that's why we need to repent.

Second Timothy 4:3-4 reveals a profound truth. "For there shall be a time when they shall not bear sound teaching, but according to their own desires, they shall heap up for themselves teachers tickling the ear, and they shall indeed turn their ears away from the Truth, and be turned aside to myths [false teachings / doctrines]."

In my mind that Scripture applied to others, but when the Father opened my eyes (as He's doing with tens of thousands), and led me to study the Scriptures from a Hebraic perspective, I began to realize just how much error I was walking in.

From Genesis to Revelation we are required to keep His Commandments and they are not burdensome. Speaking of Revelation, there are three powerful verses that show His Commandments are in our future. It's important to note, however, that these verses are referring to the Commandments found in the

Let Yahshua Rock Your World

Old Covenant because the Renewed / New Covenant was not yet compiled at the time of John's revelation.

- "And the dragon was enraged with the woman (Israel), and he went to fight with the remnant of her seed, **those guarding** [keeping/doing] **the Commands** of Elohim and possessing the witness of Yahshua Messiah" (*Revelation 12:17*).

- "Here is the endurance of the Set-Apart ones, here are **those guarding** [keeping / doing] **the Commands** of Elohim and the belief of Yahshua" (*Revelation 14:12*).

- "Blessed are **those doing His Commands**, so that the authority shall be theirs unto the tree of life, and to enter through the gates into the city" (*Revelation 22:14*).

As you can see from these passages, His true worshippers will be Commandment keepers, i.e., they will keep the Laws of Yahweh revealed in the Torah. Who will enter Yahweh's Holy City? Those who <u>DO</u> HIS COMMANDMENTS!

I was breaking the first four Commandments unknowingly.

1. **You have no other mighty ones against My face** *(Easter, Christmas, and Sun-day worship represent pagan gods)*

2. **You do not make for yourself a carved image** *(Customs associated with Christmas, Easter, and Sun-day worship, including carved statues)*

Conclusion

3. **You do not bring the Name of Yahweh your Elohim to naught** *(Bring it into non-use by replacing His Name with titles)*
4. **Remember the Sabbath day, to set it apart** *(Sun-day worship instead of resting and honoring Him on the seventh-day Sabbath)*
5. **Respect your father and your mother**
6. **You do not murder**
7. **You do not commit adultery**
8. **You do not steal**
9. **You do not bear false witness against your neighbour**
10. **You do not covet**

Yahweh is calling those who have *ears to hear* to return to Him and worship Him in Spirit and in Truth. Will you listen and respond? He's coming back soon for His Bride. Will you have oil in your lamp? Will your garments be white? Matthew 7:21-23 states:

> "Not everyone who says to Me, 'Master, Master,' shall enter into the reign of the heavens, but he who is doing the desire of My Father in the heavens. Many shall say to Me in that day, 'Master, Master, have we not prophesied in Your Name, and cast out demons in Your Name, and done many mighty works in Your Name?' And then I shall declare to

them, 'I never knew you, depart from Me, you who work lawlessness (Torahlessness)!' "

Have you ever wondered what Yahshua meant when He said, 'I never knew you?' Of course He knows us…He even knows the number of hairs on our head…He knows us before we are formed in our mother's womb; but the kind of knowing that's referred to in this Scripture is *intimacy*.

How can we develop an intimate relationship with Him? We do that by walking in His "paths of righteousness." Meet Him on the day He set apart to meet with us every week; observe His annual Festivals; eat what He declares is clean food; and proclaim His Name.

> "Therefore everyone who hears these words of Mine, and does them, shall be like a wise man who built his house on THE ROCK, and the rain came down, and the floods came, and the winds blew and beat on that house, and it did not fall, for it was founded on THE ROCK. And everyone who hears these words of Mine, and does not do them, shall be like a foolish man who built his house on the sand, and the rain came down, and the floods came, and the winds blew, and they beat on that house, and it fell, and great was its fall" (Matthew 7:21-27).

Conclusion

Let's Run to Him and Keep His Commandments!

"Thus said Yahweh, 'Guard right-ruling, and do righteousness, for near is My deliverance to come, and My righteousness to be revealed.' Blessed is the man who does this, and the son of man who lays hold on it, **guarding** [keeping / doing] **the Sabbath** lest he profane it, and guarding his hand from doing any evil. Also the sons of the **foreigner** who join themselves to Yahweh, to serve Him, and to love the Name of Yahweh, to be His servants, **all who guard** [keep / do] **the Sabbath**, and not profane it, and hold fast to My covenant – them I shall bring to My Set-Apart mountain…"
(Isaiah 56:1-2, 6-7)

"**Blessed are those <u>doing</u> His Commands**, so that the authority shall be theirs unto the tree of life, and to enter through the gates into the city."
(Revelation 22:14)

> "...and someone said to Him, 'Master, are there few who are being saved?' And He said to them, 'Strive to enter through the narrow gate, because many, I say to you, shall seek to enter in and shall not be able. When once the Master of the house has risen up and shut the door, and you begin to stand outside and knock at the door, saying, 'Master, Master, open for us,' and He shall answer and say to you, 'I do not know you, where you are from,' then you shall begin to say, 'We ate and drank in Your presence, and You taught in our streets.' But He shall say, 'I say to you I do not know you, where you are from. Depart from Me, all you workers of unrighteousness.' ' "
> (Luke 13:23-27)

Appendix 1: Hebrew Idioms

Over 140 hidden Hebrew idioms compiled from various sources. Use this guide as you study the Scriptures to find out what's hidden behind the idiom…

1st line is Book and Chapter

2nd line is Verse and Scripture

3rd line is Idiom = Meaning

Genesis, chapter 22
17: "…that I shall certainly bless you, and I shall certainly increase your **seed** as the stars of the heavens and as the sand which is on the seashore, and let your seed possess the gate of their enemies."
seed = descendants

Genesis, chapter 24
60: "And they blessed Ribqah (Rebecca) and said to her, 'Let our sister become the mother of thousands of ten thousands, and let your seed **possess the gates** of those who hate them.'"
possess the gates = capture the cities

Let Yahshua Rock Your World

Genesis, chapter 27
41: "And Ěsaw hated Ya'aqob (Jacob) because of the blessing with which his father blessed him, and Ěsaw **said in his heart**, 'The days of mourning for my father draw near, then I am going to kill my brother Ya'aqob' "
said in his heart = thought to himself

Genesis, chapter 31
35: "And she said to her father, 'Let it not displease my master that I am unable to rise before you, for **the way of women** is with me.' And he searched but did not find the house idols."
the way of women = menstruation

Genesis, chapter 40
13: "Yet, within three days Pharaoh is going to **lift up your head** and restore you to your place, and you shall put Pharaoh's cup in his hand according to the former ruling, when you were his cupbearer."
lift up your head = restore you to honor

Exodus, chapter 1
5: "And all the souls that **came out of the loins** of Jacob were seventy souls: for Joseph was in Egypt already" (KJV).
came out of the loins = descendants

Exodus, chapter 3
8: "And I am come down to deliver them out of the hand of the Egyptians, and to bring them up out of that land unto a good land and a large, unto a land **flowing with milk and honey**; unto the place of the Canaanites, and the Hittites, and the Amorites, and the Perizzites, and the Hivites, and the Jebusites."

Hebrew Idioms

flowing with milk and honey = fertile, productive

Exodus, chapter 3
19: "But I know that the sovereign of Mitsrayim (Egypt) is not going to let you go, not even by **a strong hand**."

a strong hand = a strong force

Exodus, chapter 13
2: "Set apart to Me all the first-born, the one **opening the womb** among the children of Yisra'ĕl, among man and among beast, it is Mine."

opening the womb = is born

Exodus, chapter 15
25: "Then he cried out to Yahweh, and Yahweh showed him a tree. And when he threw it into the waters, **the waters were made sweet**. There He made a law and a right-ruling for them, and there He tried them."

the waters were made sweet = water was made fit to drink

Exodus, chapter 32
19: "And it came to be, as soon as he came near the camp, that he saw the calf and the dancing. And Mosheh's **displeasure burned**, and he threw the tablets out of his hands and broke them at the foot of the mountain."

displeased burned = became very angry, his anger increased, he became incensed with anger

Exodus, chapter 34
6: "...'The LORD, The LORD God, merciful and gracious, **longsuffering**, and abundant in goodness and truth...' " (KJV).

longsuffering = patient, slow to get angry

Leviticus, chapter 20
18: "And a man who lies with a woman during **her sickness** and uncovers her nakedness: he has laid bare her flow, and she has uncovered the flow of her blood, both of them shall be cut off from the midst of their people."
her sickness = her menstrual period

Leviticus, chapter 22
6: "…the **being** who has touched it shall be unclean until evening, and does not eat the set-apart offerings, but shall bathe his body in water."
being = person

Deuteronomy, chapter 5
6: "I am Yahweh your Elohim (Mighty One) who brought you out of the land of Mitsrayim (Egypt), out of the **house of bondage**."
house of bondage = (land of) slavery

Deuteronomy, chapter 8
14: "…that **your heart then becomes lifted up**, and you forget Yahweh your Elohim who brought you out of the land of Mitsrayim (Egypt), from the house of bondage…"
your heart then becomes lifted up = you become overwhelmed with pride

Deuteronomy, chapter 15
7: "When there is a poor man with you, one of your brothers, within any of the gates in your land which Yahweh your Elohim is giving you, do not harden your heart nor **shut your hand** from your poor brother…"
shut your hand = selfishly keep

Hebrew Idioms

Deuteronomy, chapter 20

8: "And the officers shall speak further to the people, and say, 'Who is the man who is afraid and tender of heart? Let him go and return to his house, lest the heart of his brothers **faint** like his heart.'"

faint = lose courage

Deuteronomy, chapter 21

17: "But he is to acknowledge the son of the unloved wife as the first-born by giving him a double portion of all that he has, for he is **the beginning of his strength** – the right of the first-born is his."

the beginning of his strength = his first child

Deuteronomy, chapter 23

13: "…and you shall have a sharp implement among your equipment, and **when you sit down outside**, you shall dig with it and turn and cover your excrement."

when you sit down outside = defecate outside / along the way / 'en route'

Deuteronomy, chapter 28

28: "Yahweh shall smite you with madness and blindness and **bewilderment of heart**."

bewilderment of heart = blankness of mind

Joshua, chapter 10

6: "And the men of Gib'on [Gibeon] sent to Yehoshua at the camp at Gilgal, saying, 'Do not **withdraw your hand** from your servants. Come up to us quickly, and save us and help us, for all the sovereigns of the Amorites who dwell in the mountains have assembled against us.'"

withdraw your hand = do not let go, do not abandon

Judges, chapter 3

28: "And he said to them, 'Follow me, for Yahweh has **given your enemies** the Mo'abites **into your hand**.' And they went down after him, and took the fords of Yardĕn (Jordon) leading to Mo'ab, and did not allow anyone to pass over."

given your enemies into your hand = defeated your enemies for you

Judges, chapter 13

5: "For look, you are conceiving and bearing a son. And let no razor come upon his head, for the youth is a Nazirite (Nazarene) to Elohim **from the womb** on. And he shall begin to save Yisra'ĕl (Israel) out of the hand of the Philistines."

from the womb = from birth

1 Samuel, chapter 10

9: "And it came to be, when he had turned his back to go from Shemu'ĕl (Samuel), that Elohim **gave him another heart**. And all those signs came on that day."

gave him another heart = changed his attitude

1 Samuel, chapter 24

3: "And he came to the sheepcotes by the way, where was a cave; and Saul went in to **cover his feet**: and David and his men remained in the sides of the cave" (KJV).

cover his feet = relieve himself

Hebrew Idioms

1 Samuel, chapter 25
22: "So and more also do God unto the enemies of David, if I leave of all that pertain to him by the morning light **any that pisseth against the wall**" (KJV).
any that pisseth against the wall = any male, any men

2 Samuel, chapter 1
12: "And they mourned and wept and fasted until evening for Sha'ul (Saul) and for Yehonathan (Jonathan) his son, and for the people of Yahweh and for **the house of Yisra'ĕl** (Israel), because they had fallen by the sword."
the house of Israel = the nation of Israel

2 Samuel, chapter 18
25: "And the watchman cried, and told the king. And the king said, 'If he be alone, **there is tidings in his mouth**.' And he came apace, and drew near."
there is tidings in his mouth = he brings good news

1 Kings, chapter 2
10: "So David **slept with his fathers**, and was buried in the city of David."
slept with his fathers = died

2 Kings, chapter 2
7: "And **fifty men of the sons of the prophets** went, and stood to view afar off: and they two stood by Jordan."
fifty men of the sons of the prophets = a group of 50 prophets

Let Yahshua Rock Your World

2 Kings, chapter 4
29: "And he said to Gĕḥazi, '**Gird up your loins**, and take my staff in your hand, and go. When you meet anyone, do not greet him, and when anyone greets you, do not answer him. And you shall lay my staff on the face of the child.' "
gird up your loins = get ready

2 Kings, chapter 19
26: "And their inhabitants **were powerless**, they were overthrown and put to shame, they were as the grass of the field and the green plants, as the grass on the house-tops and withered before it came up."
were powerless = weak, of little strength

2 Chronicles, chapter 25
17: "And Amatsyahu (Amaziah) sovereign of Yahudah (Judah) took counsel and sent to Yo'ash (Joash) son of Yeho'aḥaz (Jehoahaz), son of Yĕhu (Jehu), sovereign of Yisra'ĕl (Israel), saying, "Come, let us **look each other in the face**!"
look each other in the face = meet each other in battle

2 Chronicles, chapter 36
13: "And he also rebelled against Sovereign Nebukadnetstsar (Nebuchadnezzar), who had made him swear by Elohim, but he **stiffened his neck** and hardened his heart against turning to Yahweh Elohim of Yisra'ĕl (Israel)."
stiffened his neck = became stubborn

Esther, chapter 1
14: "…and who were close to him: Karshena (Carshena), Shĕthar, Admatha, Tarshish, Meres, Marsena, Memukan (Memucan), the

Hebrew Idioms

seven princes of Persia and Media, who **saw the sovereign's face**, who sat first in the reign…"
saw the sovereign's face = had access to him

Esther, chapter 2
21: "In those days, while Mordekai (Mordecai) sat within the sovereign's gate, two of the sovereign's eunuchs, Bigthan and Teresh, doorkeepers, were wroth and sought to **lay hands on Sovereign** Aḥashwĕrosh."
lay hands on Soverign = assassinate

Esther, chapter 6
10: "And the sovereign said to Haman, 'Hurry, take the robe and the horse, as you have spoken, and do so for Mordekai the Yahudite (Jew) who sits in the sovereign's gate. **Let no word fail** of all that you have spoken.' "
let no word fail = neglect

Job, chapter 1
12: "And Yahweh said to Satan, 'See, all that he has is in your hand. Only **do not lay a hand on** himself.' And Satan went out from the presence of Yahweh."
do not lay a hand on = do not harm

Job, chapter 20
20: "For he shall not know **ease in his innermost**, neither save what he desires."
ease in his innermost = greedy

Job, chapter 23
16: "For Ĕl has made me **faint-hearted**, and the Almighty has alarmed me…"
faint-hearted = me fearful

Job, chapter 31
10: "…let my wife grind for another, and let others **bow down over** her."
bow down over = have sex with

Job, chapter 33
16: "…then He **opens the ears** of men, and seals their instruction…"
opens the ears = informs, reveals

Job, chapter 35
8: "Your wrong is for a man like yourself, and your righteousness for **a son of man**."
a son of man = other humans

Psalm, chapter 3
7: "Arise, O Yahweh; Save me, O my Elohim! Because You have smitten all my enemies on the cheek; You have **broken the teeth** of the wrong."
broken the teeth = make powerless

Psalm, chapter 4
1: "Answer me when I call, O Elohim of my righteousness! You **gave relief to me** when I was in distress; Show favour to me, and hear my prayer."
gave relief to me = set free

Hebrew Idioms

Psalm, chapter 5
9: "For there is no stability in their mouth; Their inward part is destruction; **Their throat is an open grave**; They flatter with their tongue."
their throat is an open grave = they speak deceitfully

Psalm, chapter 6
7: "My **eye has grown dim** because of grief; It grows old because of all my adversaries."
eye has grown dim = vision is blurred

Psalm, chapter 7
3: "O Yahweh my Elohim, if I have done this: If there is **unrighteousness in my hands**…"
unrighteousness in my hands = guilty

Psalm, chapter 7
9: "Please let the evil of the wrong be ended, And establish the righteous; For the righteous Elohim is **a trier of hearts and kidneys**."
a trier of hearts and kidneys = thoughts and emotions

Psalm, chapter 10
5: "His ways are always prosperous! Your right-rulings are on high, out of his sight! He **snorts** at all his adversaries!"
snorts = scoffs

Psalm, chapter 11
6: "Upon the wrong He rains snares, Fire and sulphur and a scorching wind Are **the portion of their cup**."
the portion of their cup = their destiny

Let Yahshua Rock Your World

Psalm, chapter 12
2: "They speak falsehood with each other; They speak with flattering lips, a **double heart**."
double heart = duplicity

Psalm, chapter 17
8: "Guard me as the **apple of Your eye**. Hide me under the shadow of Your wings…"
apple of Your eye = pupil

Psalm, chapter 24
4: "He who has **innocent hands** and a clean heart, Who did not bring his life to naught, And did not swear deceivingly."
innocent hands = pure actions

Psalm, chapter 25
1: "To You, O Yahweh, I **lift up my being**."
lift up my being = pray

Psalm, chapter 27
8: "To my heart You have said, '**Seek My face**.' Your face, Yahweh, I seek."
seek My face = seek me

Psalm, chapter 33
18: "See, **the eye of Yahweh is on** those fearing Him, On those waiting for His kindness…"
the eye of Yahweh is on = YHWH watches over

Hebrew Idioms

Psalm, chapter 41
9: "Even my own friend in whom I trusted, who ate my bread, Has **lifted up his heel against** me."
lifted up his heel against = turned against

Psalm, chapter 73
9: "They have set their mouth against the heavens, And their **tongue walks through the earth**, *saying...*"
tongue walks through the earth = arrogantly order everyone

Psalm, chapter 75
5 "**Do not lift up your horn on high** (You speak with a stiff neck)."
Do not lift up your horn on high = Do not defy Elohim

Psalm, chapter 89
13: "You have a mighty arm, Your hand is strong, Your **right hand** exalted."
right hand = might

Psalm, chapter 89
22: "No enemy subjects him to tribute, And no **son of wickedness** afflicts him."
son of wickedness = wicked person

Psalm, chapter 90
12: "Teach us to **number our days**, And let us bring the heart to wisdom."
number our days = use our time wisely

Psalm, chapter 94
9: "He who **planted** the ear, does He not hear? He who formed the eye, does He not see?"
planted = created

Psalm, chapter 102
2: "**Do not hide Your face from** me In the day of my distress; Incline Your ear to me; In the day I call, answer me speedily."
Do not hide Your face from = refuse to answer

Psalm, chapter 121
1: "I **lift up** my **eyes** to the hills; Where does my help come from?"
lift up eyes = look up toward

Psalm, chapter 124
3: "Then they would have **swallowed us alive**, In their burning rage against us…"
swallowed us alive = killed

Proverbs, chapter 17
22: "A rejoicing heart causes good healing, But a stricken spirit **dries the bones**."
dries the bones = drains strength

Proverbs, chapter 18
20: "A man's stomach is satisfied From the **fruit of his mouth**; He is satisfied with the increase of his lips."
fruit of his mouth = his words

Hebrew Idioms

Proverbs, chapter 24
20: "For there is no future for the evil-doer; **The lamp** of the wrongdoers **is put out**."
The lamp is put out = will die

Song of Solomon, chapter 2
4: "He brought me to the banqueting house, and **his banner over me was love**" (KJV).
his banner over me was love = he loved me very much

Song of Solomon, chapter 2
17: "**Until the day breaks** and the shadows have fled, Turn, my beloved, And be like a gazelle or a young stag on the mountains of Bether."
until the day breaks = until dawn

Song of Solomon, chapter 4
2: "Thy teeth are like a flock of sheep that are even shorn, which came up from the washing; whereof every one bear twins, and **none is barren** among them" (KJV).
none is barren = none is missing

Isaiah, chapter 9
9: "And the people shall know, all of them, Ephrayim (Ephraim) and the inhabitant of Shomeron (Samaria), who say in pride and **greatness of heart**…"
greatness of heart = arrogant

Let Yahshua Rock Your World

Isaiah, chapter 14
12: "How you have fallen from the heavens, O Hělěl (Lucifer), **son of the morning**! You have been cut down to the ground, you who laid low the gentiles!"
son of the morning = morning star

Isaiah, chapter 35
10: "And the ransomed of the LORD shall return, and come to Zion with songs and everlasting **joy upon their heads**: they shall obtain joy and gladness, and sorrow and sighing shall flee away" (KJV).
joy upon their heads = they will be joyful

Isaiah, chapter 52
7: "How pleasant upon the mountains are the **feet** of him who brings good news, who proclaims peace, who brings good news, who proclaims deliverance, who says to Tsiyon (Zion), 'Your Elohim reigns!'"
feet = person

Isaiah, chapter 57
4: "Against whom are you sporting? Against whom do you **make a wide mouth** and stick out the tongue? Are you not children of transgression, offspring of falsehood..."
make a wide mouth = sneer

Isaiah, chapter 60
16: "And you shall **drink dry the milk of the gentiles**, and shall milk the breast of sovereigns. And you shall know that I, Yahweh, your Saviour and your Redeemer, am the Elohim of Ya'aqob (Jacob)."
drink the milk of the gentiles = receive the wealth of other countries

Hebrew Idioms

Isaiah, chapter 61
3: "to appoint unto those who mourn in Tsiyon (Zion): to give them embellishment for ashes, **the oil of joy** for mourning, the garment of praise for the spirit of heaviness. And they shall be called trees of righteousness, a planting of Yahweh, to be adorned."
the oil of joy = joy

Jeremiah, chapter 4
4: "Circumcise yourselves unto Yahweh, and **take away the foreskins of your hearts**, you men of Yahudah (Judah) and inhabitants of Yerushalayim (Jerusalem), lest My wrath come forth like fire and burn, with none to quench it, because of the evil of your deeds."
take away the foreskins of your heart = dedicate yourselves fully to Elohim

Jeremiah, chapter 4
19: "**My bowels, my bowels**! I am pained at my very heart; my heart maketh a noise in me; I cannot hold my peace, because thou hast heard, O my soul, the sound of the trumpet, the alarm of war" (KJV).
My bowels, my bowels = pain

Jeremiah, chapter 4
30: "And when you are ravaged, what would you do? Though you put on crimson, though you adorn yourself with ornaments of gold, though you enlarge your eyes with paint, you adorn yourself in vain. Your lovers despise you, they **seek your life**."
seek your life = want to kill you

Let Yahshua Rock Your World

Jeremiah, chapter 5
5: " 'Let me go to the great men and speak to them, for they have known the way of Yahweh, the right-ruling of their Elohim.' But these have altogether **broken the yoke** and torn off the bonds."
broken the yoke = rejected Elohim's authority

Jeremiah, chapter 6
10: "To whom shall I speak and give warning, so that they hear? See, **their ear is uncircumcised**, and they are unable to listen. See, the word of Yahweh is a reproach to them, they do not delight in it."
their ear is uncircumcised = they don't listen

Jeremiah, chapter 7
12: "But go now to My place at Shiloh, **where I set My Name at the first**, and see what I did to it because of the evil of My people Yisra'ĕl (Israel)."
where I set my name at the first = where I chose to be worshiped

Jeremiah, chapter 9
1: "Oh, that my head were **waters**, and my eyes a fountain of tears, and I would weep day and night for the slain of the daughter of my people!"
waters = spring of water

Jeremiah, chapter 25
15: "For thus said Yahweh Elohim of Yisra'ĕl (Israel) to me, 'Take this **wine cup of wrath** from My hand, and make all the nations, to whom I send you, drink it.' "
wine cup of wrath = my anger

Hebrew Idioms

Jeremiah, chapter 50
33: "Thus said Yahweh of hosts, '**The children** of Yisra'ĕl (Israel) were oppressed, along with the children of Yahudah (Judah). And all who took them captive have held them fast, they refused to let them go.' "
The children = people of

Jeremiah, chapter 51
37: "And Babel shall become a heap, a habitation of jackals, an astonishment and **a hissing**, without inhabitant."
a hissing = a scorn

Lamentations, chapter 1
16: "This is why I weep. My eye, my **eye is running down with water**, Because the comforter, Who could bring back my life, Has been far from me. My children are stunned, For the enemy has prevailed."
eye is running down with water = eyes flow with tears

Ezekiel, chapter 3
7: "But the house of Yisra'ĕl (Israel) is going to refuse to listen to you, for they refuse to listen to Me. For all the house of Yisra'ĕl are **hard of head**, and hard of heart."
hard of head = stubborn

Ezekiel, chapter 16
25: "You built your high places at the head of every way, and made your loveliness to be loathed. And you **parted your feet** to everyone who passed by, and increased your whorings."
parted your feet = offer self for sex

Ezekiel, chapter 16
26: "And you whored with the sons of Mitsrayim (Egypt), your neighbours, **great of flesh**. And you increased your whorings to provoke Me."
great of flesh = lustful

Malachi, chapter 1
11: " 'For from the rising of the sun, even to its going down, My Name is great among nations. And in every place incense is presented to My Name, and a clean offering. For **My Name** is great among nations,' said Yahweh of hosts."
My Name = me

Malachi, chapter 2
12: "The LORD will cut off the man that doeth this, **the master and the scholar**, out of the tabernacles of Jacob, and him that offereth an offering unto the LORD of hosts" (KJV).
the master and the scholar = every single person

Matthew, chapter 1
18: "Now the birth of Jesus Christ was on this wise: When as his mother Mary was espoused to Joseph, before they came together, **she was found with child** of the Holy Ghost" (KJV).
she was found with child = was pregnant

Matthew, chapter 3
8: "**Bear, therefore, fruits** worthy of repentance…"
Bear, therefore, fruits = produce results

Hebrew Idioms

Matthew, chapter 5

17: "Think not that I am come **to destroy the law, or the prophets**: I am not come to destroy, but to fulfill. 18: For verily I say unto you, Till heaven and earth pass, one jot or one tittle shall in no wise pass from the law, till all be fulfilled" (KJV).

to destroy the law, or the prophets = Correctly interpreted the law and prophets

Matthew, chapter 6

22: "The lamp of the body is the eye. **If** therefore **your eye is good**, all your body shall be enlightened."

if your eye is good = if you are generous

Matthew, chapter 6

23: "But **if your eye is evil**, all your body shall be darkened. If, then, the light that is within you is darkness, how great is that darkness!"

if your eye is evil = if your are stingy

Matthew, chapter 8

12: "…but the sons of the reign shall be cast out into **outer darkness** – there shall be weeping and gnashing of teeth."

outer darkness = a place away from righteous

Matthew, chapter 10

27: "What I say to you in the dark, speak in the light. And **what you hear in the ear**, proclaim on the house-tops."

what you hear in the ear = what you hear in secret

Matthew, chapter 10
38: "And **he who does not take up his stake** and follow after Me is not worthy of Me."
he who does not take up his stake = does not follow Messiah's Torah interpretation

Matthew, chapter 11
15: "**He who has ears to hear, let him hear!**"
He who has ears to hear, let him hear! = Everyone should listen carefully

Matthew, chapter 22
16: "And they sent to Him their taught ones with the Herodians, saying, 'Teacher, we know that You are true, and teach the way of Elohim in truth, and it does not concern You about anyone, for You are **not partial to any man**.'"
not partial to any man = you do not judge on outward signs

Matthew, chapter 23
32: "…and **you fill up the measure of your fathers!**"
you fill up the measure of your fathers = Finish what was started

Mark, chapter 1
32: "And at even, when the sun did set, they brought unto him **all that were diseased**, and them that were possessed with devils" (KJV).
all that were diseased = Those who were sick

Hebrew Idioms

Mark, chapter 2
19: "And Yahshua said to them, 'Are the **friends of the bridegroom** able to fast while the bridegroom is with them? As long as they have the bridegroom with them they are not able to fast.'"
friends of the bridegroom = Guests of the bridegroom

Mark, chapter 3
21: "And when **his friends** heard of it, they went out to lay hold on him: for they said, He is beside himself" (KJV).
his friends = His family

Mark, chapter 9
1: "And He said to them, 'Truly, I say to you that there are some standing here who shall not **taste of death** at all until they see the reign of Elohim having come in power…'"
taste of death = die

Luke, chapter 6
22: "Blessed are you when men shall hate you, and when they shall cut you off, and shall reproach you, and **cast out your name as wicked**, for the sake of the Son of Adam."
cast out your name as wicked = publish false information about you

Luke, chapter 16
22: "And it came to be that the beggar died, and was carried by the messengers to the **bosom of Abraham**. And the rich man also died and was buried."
bosom of Abraham = Be with Abraham, heaven

Let Yahshua Rock Your World

John, chapter 1
16: "And out of His completeness we all did receive, and **favour upon favour**…"
favour upon favour = Blessing after blessing, very blessed

John, chapter 2
4: "…said to her, 'Woman, **what is that to Me** and to you? My hour has not yet come.' "
what is that to Me = What does that have to do with us?

John, chapter 9
24: "So for the second time they called the man who was blind, and said to him, '**Give esteem to Elohim**, we know that this Man is a sinner.' "
Give esteem to Elohim = To promise under oath to Elohim

John, chapter 20
26: "And after eight days His taught ones were again inside, and T'oma (Thomas) with them. Yahshua came, the doors having been shut, and He stood in the midst, and said, '**Peace to you!**' "
Peace to you = Hello! Literally "shalom alechiem"

Acts, chapter 11
22: "And word of it **came to the ears of the assembly** in Yerushalayim (Jerusalem), and they sent out Barnabah (Barnabas) to go as far as Antioch…"
came to the ears of the assembly = The people heard about it

Hebrew Idioms

Acts, chapter 15
10: "Now then, why do you try Elohim by **putting a yoke on the neck** of the taught ones which neither our fathers nor we were able to bear?"
putting a yoke on the neck = burden with obligations

Acts, chapter 17
21: "For all the Athenians and the strangers living there **spent their leisure** time in doing naught but to speak or to hear what is fresh."
spent their leisure = spending time

Acts, chapter 18
6: "However, when they resisted and blasphemed, he shook his garments and said to them, '**Your blood is upon your head**, I am clean. From now on I shall go to the gentiles.' "
Your blood is upon your own head = You take the blame

Acts, chapter 18
14: "And as Sha'ul (Paul) was about **to open his mouth**, Gallion (Gallio) said to the Yahudim (Jews), 'If it were a matter of wrongdoing or wicked recklessness, O Yahudim (Jews), there would be reason why I should bear with you.' "
to open his mouth = to speak

Acts, chapter 20
33: "I have coveted no man's **silver, or gold**, or apparel."
silver, or gold = Money

Let Yahshua Rock Your World

Acts, chapter 22
14: "And he said, 'The Elohim of our fathers has appointed you to know His desire, and to see the Righteous One, and to hear **the voice from His mouth**.' "
the voice of His mouth = hear him speak

Acts, chapter 26
14: "And when we had all fallen to the ground, I heard a voice speaking to me, and saying in the Hebrew language, 'Sha'ul (Paul), Sha'ul (Paul), why do you persecute Me? It is hard for you to **kick against the prods**.' "
kick against the prods = hurt oneself by active resistance

Acts, chapter 28
27: "…for the heart of this people has become thickened, and with their **ears they heard heavily**, and they have closed their eyes, lest they should see with their eyes and hear with their ears, and understand with their heart, and turn back, and I should heal them."
ears they heard heavily = be slow to understand

Romans, chapter 1
17: "For in it the righteousness of Elohim is revealed **from belief to belief**, as it has been written, 'But the righteous shall live by belief.' "
from belief to belief = from start to finish

Romans, chapter 12
9: "**Let love be without dissimulation**. Abhor that which is evil; cleave to that which is good" (KJV).
let love be without dissimulation = Love without hypocrisy

Hebrew Idioms

Romans, chapter 12
20: "Instead, if your enemy hungers, feed him; if he thirsts, give him a drink, for in so doing you shall **heap coals of fire on his head**."
heap coals of fire on his head = be very kind to

1 Corinthians, chapter 7
35: "And this I speak for your own profit; not that I may **cast a snare upon** you, but for that which is comely, and that ye may attend upon the Lord without distraction" (KJV).
cast a snare upon = restrict, control

1 Corinthians, chapter 14
9: "So also you, if you do not give speech by the tongue that is clear, how shall it be known what is spoken? For you shall be **speaking into the air**."
speaking into the air = talking with no one understanding

1 Corinthians, chapter 15
40: "And there are **heavenly bodies** and earthly bodies, but the esteem of the heavenly is truly one, and the esteem of the earthly is another..."
heavenly bodies = celestial objects

2 Corinthians, chapter 3
18: "And we all, as with unveiled face we see as in a mirror the esteem of Yahweh, are being transformed into the same likeness **from esteem to esteem**, as from Yahweh, the Spirit."
from esteem to esteem = becoming more like Yahweh

Ephesians, chapter 1
23: "...which is His body, the **completeness of Him who fills all in all**."

completeness of Him who fills all in all = YHWH is everywhere, omnipresent

Colossians, chapter 1
23: "…if indeed you continue in the belief, founded and steadfast, and are not moved away from the expectation of the Good News which you heard, which was proclaimed to every creature **under the heaven**, of which I, Sha'ul (Paul), became a servant…"
under the heaven = on earth

2 Thessalonians, chapter 3
12: "But we command and urge such, through our Master Yahshua Messiah, to settle down, work and **eat their own bread**."
eat their own bread = work for a living

Hebrews, chapter 8
9: "…not according to the covenant that I made with their fathers in the day when **I took them by the hand** to lead them out of the land of Mitsrayim (Egypt), because they did not continue in My covenant, and I disregarded them," says Yahweh."
I took them by the hand = I guided them carefully

Hebrews, chapter 12
28: "Therefore, receiving an unshakeable reign, **let us hold the favour**, through which we serve Elohim pleasingly with reverence and awe…"
let us hold the favour = let us be thankful

James, chapter 1
23: "For if any be a hearer of the word, and not a doer, he is like unto a man beholding **his natural face** in a glass…" (KJV)

Hebrew Idioms

his natural face = his natural face

James, chapter 3

6: "And the tongue is a fire, the world of unrighteousness. Among our members the tongue is set, the one defiling the entire body, and setting on fire **the wheel of life**, and it is set on fire by Gehenna."
the wheel of life = Cycle of life

1 Peter, chapter 1

13: "Therefore, having **girded up the loins of your mind**, being sober, set your expectation perfectly upon the favour that is to be brought to you at the revelation of Yahshua Messiah…"
girded up the loins of your mind = prepare your thoughts

Jude, verse 13

13: "…wild waves of the sea foaming up their own shame, straying stars for whom **blackness of darkness** is kept forever."
blackness of darkness = gloomy sheol

Revelation, chapter 16

3: "And the second angel poured out his vial upon the sea; and it became as the blood of a dead man: and every **living soul** died in the sea" (KJV).
living soul = living creature

Revelation, chapter 20

10: "And the devil, who led them astray, was thrown into the **lake of fire** and sulphur where the beast and the false prophet are. And they shall be tortured day and night forever and ever."
lake of fire = place of destruction

Let Yahshua Rock Your World

> "Yahweh looked down from the heavens on the sons of mankind, To see if there is a wise one, seeking Yahweh."
> (Psalm 14:2)

Appendix 2: Sabbath to Sunday

A well-known expert on the Sabbath is Dr. Samuele Bacchiocchi, a retired theology professor at Andrews University in Michigan.

Bacchiocchi earned his doctorate in Church History at the Pontifical Georgian University in Rome. At that university he not only had open access to long-forgotten historical records, he also graduated at the top of his class – *summa cum laude*, an honor which included a gold medal from Pope Paul VI for his class work and dissertation, "From Sabbath to Sunday: A Historical Investigation of the Rise of Sunday Observance in Early Christianity."

What he found in that investigation would probably shock most Christians who have never studied the subject, nor thought deeply about what became of the Fourth Commandment.

Bacchiocchi believes anti-Judaism caused the abandonment of the Sabbath, and pagan sun worship influenced the adoption of Sunday as there's no Scriptural mandate to change or eliminate Sabbath-keeping, and he singles out the Catholic Church for its role in changing the day.

He says evidence of anti-Judaism is found in the writings of Christian leaders such as Ignatius, Barnabas and Justin in the second century. He notes these three "witnessed and participated in the process of separation from Judaism which led the majority of the Christians to abandon the Sabbath and adopt Sunday as the new day of worship."

Here's what Constantine said in his letter written in A.D. 325:

> "Let us then have nothing in common with the detestable Jewish crowd: for we have received from our Savior a different way ... Strive and pray continually that the purity of your souls may not seem in anything to be sullied by fellowship with the customs of these most wicked men ... All should unite in desiring that which sound reason appears to demand and in avoiding all participation in the perjured conduct of the Jews."

Not surprisingly, anti-Sabbath laws followed in Rome – imposing harsh penalties for anyone who refused to work on Saturday or who deigned to worship on that day of the week.

He quotes Sylvester I, the pope from 314-337:

> "If every Sunday is to be observed joyfully by the Christians on account of the resurrection, then every Sabbath on account of the burial is to be execration (loathing or cursing) of the Jews."

Sabbath to Sunday

Observing the Sabbath meant excommunication from the Church as of A.D. 363 and the Council of Laodicea:

> "Christians must not judaize by resting on the Sabbath, but must work on that day, rather honoring the Lord's Day; and, if they can, resting then as Christians. But if any shall be found to be judaizers, let them be anathema from Christ."

But Bacchiocchi also reminds readers the Saturday Sabbath, despite official repression against it, never was completely abandoned.

Likewise, over the years, some prominent voices have never forgotten the Sabbath – and what became of it.

Was it, indeed, a Roman Catholic decision made after the first century and the death of the apostles? It's hard to argue with the historical record. In fact, some Catholics revel in the role Rome played in the switch.

> "The Catholic Church of its own infallible authority created Sunday a holy day to take the place of the Sabbath of the old law," wrote the Kansas City Catholic on Feb. 9, 1893.

Other Catholic sources agree with little self-doubt.

> "Sunday is a Catholic institution, and its claims to observance can be defended only on Catholic principles," wrote the Catholic Press in Sydney, Australia, on Aug. 25, 1900. "From beginning to end of Scripture there is not a single passage that

warrants the transfer of weekly public worship from the last day of the week to the first."

James Cardinal Gibbons seconds the motion in his famous book "The Faith of Our Fathers," published in 1876:

> "You may read the Bible from Genesis to Revelation, and you will not find a single line authorizing the sanctification of Sunday. The Scriptures enforce the religious observance of Saturday, a day which we never sanctify."

But it's not just Catholics who acknowledge the Church has just plain forgotten one of Elohim's Great Commandments – without so much as a second thought.

Dwight L. Moody, one of America's great Protestant evangelists of the 19th century, noted the omission in his book, "Weighed and Wanting."

> "The Sabbath was binding in Eden, and it has been in force ever since," he wrote. "The fourth commandment begins with the word 'remember,' showing that the Sabbath already existed when God wrote the law on the tablets of stone at Sinai. How can men claim that this one commandment has been done away with when they will admit that the other nine are still binding?"

There is also evidence that the early disciples kept the Sabbath on the true day:

"The primitive Christians did keep the Sabbath...in which some portion of the Law was read: and this continued till the time of the Laodicean council." The Whole Works of Jeremey Taylor, Vol. IX, p416 (R. Heber's Edition, Vol. XII, p.416)

"The ancient Christians were very careful in the observation of Saturday, or the seventh day. It is plain that all the Oriental churches, and the greatest part of the world, observed the Sabbath as a festival...Athanasius likewise tells us that they held religious assemblies on the Sabbath, not because they were infected with Judaism, but to worship [Yahushua], the [Master] of the Sabbath, Epiphanius says the same." Antiquities of the Christian Church, Vol. II, Book XX, chap. 3, Sec. 1, 66.1137, 1138

"Ambrose, the celebrated bishop of Milan, said that when he was in Milan he observed Saturday, but when in Rome observed Sunday. This gave rise to the proverb 'When you are in Rome, do as Rome does,' " Heylyn, The History of the Sabbath, 1613.

Constantine later enforced keeping a Sabbath on the first day of the week, which he calls "the venerable day of the sun." Venerable means 'commanding respect'.

The text of Constantine's Sunday law of 321 A.D. is:

"On the venerable day of the Sun, let the magistrates and people residing in cities rest, and let all workshops be closed. In the country however persons engaged in agriculture may freely and lawfully continue their pursuits because it often happens that another day is not suitable for gain-sowing or vine planting; lest by neglecting the proper moment for such operations the bounty of heaven should be lost."

Later, those who observed the Sabbath were persecuted and killed by the Catholic Church. When the Jesuit St. Francis Xavier arrived in India he immediately requested to the pope to set up the Inquisition there.

"The Jewish wickedness" of which Xavier complained was evidently the Sabbath-keeping among those native Christians as we shall see in our next quotation. When one of these Sabbath-keeping Christians was taken by the Inquisition he was accused of having *Judaized*; which means having conformed to the ceremonies of the Mosaic Law; such as not eating pork, hare, fish without scales, of having attended the solemnization of the Sabbath. Account of the Inquisition at Goa, Dellon, p.56. London, 1815

"Of an hundred persons condemned to be burnt as Jews, there are scarcely four who profess that faith at their death; the rest exclaiming and protesting to their last gasp that they are Christians, and have been so during their whole lives" (Ibid p.64).

Today, some of the leading Baptists even have admitted that the Sunday Sabbath isn't in the scriptures:

> "There was and is a commandment to keep holy the Sabbath day, but that Sabbath day was not on Sunday...It will be said, however, and with some show of triumph, that the Sabbath was transferred from the seventh to the first day of the week....where can the record of such a transaction be found? Not in the New Covenant. Of course, I quite well know that Sunday did come into use in early Christian history as a religious day, as we learn from the Christian Fathers and other sources. But what a pity that it comes branded with the mark of paganism, and christened with the name of a sun god, when adopted and sanctioned by the papal apostasy, and bequeathed as a sacred legacy to Protestantism!" *Dr. Edward Hiscox*, author of The Baptist Manual.

There's no place like Rome

As Christianity spread through the pagan Roman Empire, it was finally given official toleration in the year 312 by Emperor Constantine, who purportedly had a vision that prompted his soldiers to fight under a "symbol of Christ," leading to a key military victory. The emperor then restored confiscated church property and even offered public funds to churches in need.

Sunday observance received a historic boost when Constantine – himself a pagan who is said to have adopted Christianity at least nominally – established Sunday as the first day of the week in the Roman calendar and issued a mandatory order prohibiting work on that day, in honor of the sun god.

On March 7, 321, he decreed, "On the venerable day of the Sun, let the magistrates and people residing in cities rest, and let all workshops be closed." Farmers were given an exception.

"The importance of the actions of Constantine cannot be overstated," says author Richard Rives in "Too Long in the Sun." "During his reign, pagan sun worship was blended with the worship of the Creator, and officially entitled 'Christianity.' "

Before the end of the 4th century, Sunday observance prevailed over Saturday.

In 380, Emperor Theodosius made Sunday-keeping Catholic Christianity the official religion of the empire, outlawing all other faiths:

> "We authorize the followers of this law to assume the title Catholic Christians; but as for the others, since in our judgment they are foolish madmen, we decree that they shall be branded with the ignominious name of heretics."

Sabbath to Sunday

Once Sunday had the imperial power of the Roman Catholic government behind it, Saturday Sabbath-keepers became less visible, though some Sabbatarian websites have documented mentions of seventh-day observers through the centuries.

For example, the Catholic Church persecuted Sabbath-keepers in the 15th century. At the Catholic Provincial Council of Bergen, Norway, in 1435, it was said:

> "We are informed that some people in different districts of the kingdom, have adopted and observed Saturday-keeping.
>
> It is severely forbidden – in holy church canon – [for] one and all to observe days excepting those which the holy pope, archbishop, or the bishops command. Saturday-keeping must under no circumstances be permitted hereafter further that the church canon commands. Therefore we counsel all the friends of God throughout all Norway who want to be obedient towards the holy church to let this evil of Saturday-keeping alone; and the rest we forbid under penalty of severe church punishment to keep Saturday holy."

The Catholic Encyclopedia even refers to Sabbath-keeping as "the superstitious observance of Saturday," noting it was forbidden by that council.

Most biblical scholars have little disagreement when asked what day the Bible specifically calls the Sabbath.

"The seventh day, Saturday," says, Richard Bauckham, Professor of New Testament at the University of St. Andrews in Scotland. "No other day is called the Sabbath in Old or New Covenants." ("Anti-Judaism at root of 'Sunday Sabbath'? 4th century church banned observing Saturday at risk of excommunication." WorldNetDaily. Ed. Joe Knovacs. 16 Mar 2008: 347. www.wnd.com/index.php?fa=PAGE.view&pageId=58526.)

Appendix 3:
The Disciples Kept the Sabbath

85 Times in the book of Acts

There are many Scriptures that verify the Sabbath Day being the 7th day of the week. All throughout the 'Renewed / New Covenant,' the first day of the week is called "The first day of the week" and the 7th day of the week is called "The Sabbath". This fact alone should prove when the Sabbath truly is.

However, let us examine the pattern of the disciples after Yahshua's resurrection in the book of Acts to determine what day that they attended Sabbath Services and what day they expected others to observe. We will keep a count of how many times the Sabbath is observed.

We see one example in Acts 17:1-4.

> Acts 17:1-4 (NKJV), "Now when they had passed through Amphipolis and Apollonia, they came to Thessalonica, where there was a synagogue of the

Jews (Yahudim). Then Paul, as his custom was, went in to them, and for three Sabbaths reasoned with them from the Scriptures, explaining and demonstrating that the Messiah had to suffer and rise again from the dead, and [saying], 'This Yahshua whom I preach to you is the Messiah.' And some of them were persuaded; and a great multitude of the devout Greeks, and not a few of the leading women, joined Paul and Silas."

Here we see that Paul went to a Sabbath service where there were both Yahudim (Jews) and Greeks. The Scripture also mentions that this was a regular custom of Paul. Was this also the custom of Yahshua the Messiah?

Luke 4:16, "And He came to Natsareth, where He had been brought up. And according to His practice, He went into the congregation on the Sabbath day, and stood up to read."

So here we can see that 22 years after Yahshua's death and resurrection the disciples were attending Sabbath Services. In no place do we see Paul or any other disciple teaching them that they should come back the next day for a 'first day of the week' service. But they went to three Sabbath Services where there were both Yahudim (Jews) and Greeks present. So then the doctrine that says the Yahudim (Jews) have their day (the 7th day) and the Gentiles have their day (the 1st day) is foreign to Scripture.

The Disciples Kept the Sabbath

Some would argue that Paul was at the synagogue only because that is where he would find people to witness to...not to observe the Sabbath. But the Scripture does not say that. This is an assumption that those who refuse the simplicity of the Scriptures want to make, not one that the Scriptures support. Again, the Seventh Day is called "The Sabbath Day" in this passage.

So let's see where we are at now.

Seventh day - 3 | First day - 0

Another example is found in Acts 13:13-15.

> Acts 13:13-15, "And having put out from Paphos, Sha'ul (Paul) and those with him came to Perge in Pamphulia. And Yoḥanan (John), having left them, returned to Yerushalayim (Jerusalem). But passing through from Perge, they came to Antioch in Pisidia, and went into the congregation on the Sabbath day and sat down. And after the reading of the Torah and the Prophets, the rulers of the congregation sent to them, saying, 'Men, brothers, if you have any word of encouragement for the people, speak.' "

So here is another example where Paul and the other disciples came to the Synagogue in Perge to attend the Sabbath Service.

Seventh day - 4 | First day - 0

A little later in the chapter, after Paul shares Yahshua with them we see that the Gentiles were quite interested.

> Acts 13:42, "And when the Yahudim (Jews) went out of the congregation, the gentiles begged to have these words spoken to them the next Sabbath."

Now here is a <u>perfect</u> situation for Paul to tell these Gentiles "Hey just come back tomorrow, we keep the Sabbath on the first day now!" But we don't see this written anywhere in Scripture.

> Acts 13:43-44, "And when the *meeting* of the congregation had broken up, many of the Yahudim and of the worshipping converts followed Sha'ul (Paul) and Barna<u>b</u>ah (Barnabas), who, speaking to them, were urging them to continue in the favour of Elohim. And on the next Sabbath almost all the city came together to hear the Word of Elohim."

So here is the fifth time that the disciples attended a Sabbath service on the day that Yahweh sanctified at creation. Again, the Seventh Day is called "The Sabbath" in this passage.

Seventh day - 5 | First day - 0

Here is another example in Acts 16:11-13:

> Acts 16:11-13, "Therefore, sailing from Troas, we ran a straight course to Samothrake (Samothracia), and the next day came to Neapolis, and from there to Philippi, which is the principal city of that part of Makedonia (Macedonia), a colony. And we were

The Disciples Kept the Sabbath

> staying in that city for some days. And on the Sabbath day we went outside the city by a river, where there used to be prayer. And having sat down we were speaking to the women who met there."

It was the custom of the Yahudim (Jews) of that day for the rabbi to shut down the synagogue if there were not at least 10 men that would show up for the Sabbath meeting. This could very well be why there were women meeting by the riverside for prayer. Nevertheless, we see that the disciples sought a place to meet for the Sabbath and they did. Again, the Seventh Day is called "The Sabbath Day" in this passage.

Seventh day - 6 | First day - 0

Here is another example in Acts 18:1-4:

> Acts 18:1-4, "And after this Sha'ul (Paul) left Athens and went to Corinth. And he found a certain Yahudite (Jew) named Aqulas, born in Pontos, who had recently come from Italy with his wife Priscilla – because Claudius had commanded all the Yahudim (Jews) to leave Rome – and he came to them. And because he was of the same trade, he stayed with them and was working, for they were tentmakers by trade. And he was reasoning in the congregation every Sabbath, and won over both Yahudim and Greeks."

So we see that Paul worked on the other days as a tentmaker...but on the Sabbath he did not work. And here again we see that both Yahudim (Jews) and Greeks are in the synagogue and on the Sabbath. Paul also is among them attending the Sabbath Services. The interesting thing about this verse is that instead of the Scripture saying that they attended only one or three Sabbath Services, it says that he was there <u>every Sabbath</u> persuading both Yahudim (Jews) and Greeks. Again, the Seventh Day is called "The Sabbath" in this passage so we know that we can at least count one. Let's do that.

Seventh day - 7 | First day - 0

Now if Paul was in Corinth and was reasoning in the synagogue every Sabbath, if we could find out how long he stayed in Corinth then we would know how many Sabbaths he actually attended. Let's look further.

> Acts 18:5-11, "And when Sila (Silas) and Timothy came down from Makedonia (Macedonia), Sha'ul (Paul) was pressed by the Spirit, and earnestly witnessed to the Yahudim (Jews) that Yahshua is the Messiah. However, when they resisted and blasphemed, he shook his garments and said to them, 'Your blood is upon your head, I am clean. From now on I shall go to the gentiles.' And having left there he came to the house of a certain man named Justus, who worshipped Elohim, whose house was next to the congregation. And Crispus, the ruler of the

The Disciples Kept the Sabbath

congregation, did believe in the Master with all his household. And many of the Corinthians, hearing, believed and were immersed. And the Master spoke to Sha'ul (Paul) in the night by a vision, 'Do not be afraid, but speak, and do not be silent, because I am with you, and no one shall attack you to do you evil, because I have much people in this city.' And he remained a year and six months, teaching the Word of Yahweh among them."

A year and six months! Finally the ruler of the synagogue was converted to Yahshua and Paul was there a year and six months! So the Scripture says that Paul was there every Sabbath and that he was there for a year and six months. If we counted this by our present calendar that would give us 52 Sabbaths in a year plus 26 Sabbaths in the following six months which gives us a total of 78 Sabbaths! Now let's add this to our present total:

Seventh Day - 85 | First day - 0

So we can see that the disciples observed the Sabbath and attended a Sabbath Service 85 times in the book of Acts alone! Again, the Seventh Day is called "The Sabbath" in this passage.

Nowhere in the Renewed / New Covenant writings will you find **ANYONE** (including Yahshua and His Apostles), ever changing the Seventh Day Sabbath to the first day of the week…neither **before** nor **after** His Resurrection. They **ALL** assembled on the Seventh Day Sabbath as instructed in Yahweh's Set-Apart (Holy) Written Word.

Let Yahshua Rock Your World

QUESTION:

Since it is obvious that Yahshua, the Apostles and even the Gentiles assembled on the Sabbath and *not* on the first day of the week, you have to ask yourself (just like I did) "Why do I assemble on the first day of the week?" IF I am **WALKING** in His footsteps and desiring to be **OBEDIENT** to His Written Word, then shouldn't I be **DOING** what He did? Shouldn't I observe the Sabbath the same as Yahshua, the Apostles and the Gentiles?

To believe or even entertain the idea or belief that the Sabbath is **ONLY** for the Yahudim (Jews), without one shred of Scriptural evidence, is proof of a *strong delusion.* Even the Gentiles came to the assembly on the Sabbath as previously noted above in Acts 13:42.

Keeping Yahweh's Sabbath is His **"MARK"** upon those who are His obedient children. That being said, whose mark is Sun-god-day? Currently, He has many disobedient children, but The Day **IS** coming when **EVERYONE** will keep His Sabbath. No exceptions! Don't you think it would be a good thing to start keeping His Sabbath and obeying His Word before **THAT DAY** arrives?

Those who are obedient to keeping His Sabbaths **ARE BLESSED**. By *"Sabbaths,"* I am speaking of the weekly Sabbath as well as Yahweh's other Appointed Times—His Feast Days.

The Disciples Kept the Sabbath

Choose you this day whom you will serve – Yahweh wants obedient children.

If you love Him, keep His Sabbaths!

> "Repent, for the reign of the heavens has come near!"
> (Matthew 3:2; 4:17)

Appendix 4: Old Covenant Found in the New Covenant

The Renewed / New Covenant is about ¼ of the whole Bible. For example, in one translation there are 1,221 pages in the Old Covenant and 332 pages in the Renewed / New Covenant.

Since the Renewed / New Covenant was not in existence during the time of Yahshua and the Apostles, they quoted from the Old Covenant.

There are at least 627 references to the Old Covenant in the Renewed / New Covenant.

Listed below is the number of references to the Old Covenant in each book of the Renewed / New Covenant:

Matthew: 87
Mark: 39
Luke: 43
John: 21
Acts: 57
Romans: 79
1 Corinthians: 17
2 Corinthians: 17
Galatians: 11
1 Timothy: 3
2 Timothy: 8
Titus: 4
Philemon: 1
Hebrews: 75
James: 17
1 Peter: 30
2 Peter: 3
1 John: 22

Let Yahshua Rock Your World

        Ephesians: 12   2 John: 0
        Philippians: 6   3 John: 2
        Colossians: 3   Jude: 17
        1 Thessalonians: 1   Revelation: 46
        2 Thessalonians: 6

    The Renewed / New Covenant didn't replace the Old Covenant. The correct interpretation for New Covenant is "renewed" or "refreshed." There is a "new" moon every month, but it doesn't mean that the moon has replaced the previous month. We re-new our driver's licenses every few years and say that our license is new. It's that same idea with the Old and Renewed / New Covenant's. The Old was written on stone and the Renewed/New is written on our hearts by the Spirit.

    As Brad Scott would say, "The New Covenant is not *new*, it's just *true*." It has also been said that the Old Covenant is the Renewed/New Covenant concealed and the Renewed / New Covenant is the Old Covenant revealed. The end is revealed right out of the beginning!

Appendix 5: Sabbath Around the World

Dr. William Meade Jones lived over a hundred and fifty years ago, and was a well-known London, England, research expert. He discovered in his studies that the Seventh-day Sabbath was the only weekly Sabbath ever commanded by Elohim in the Bible

Jones decided that, since Scripture clearly shows that the Bible Sabbath was first given to mankind at the end of the Creation Week, (Genesis 2:1-3) then two important facts would have had to be known throughout the ancient world: First, a fixing of the seven-day weekly cycle on a world-wide basis, and second, an ancient world-wide knowledge of the Seventh-day Sabbath.

Jones was convinced of this for several reasons: Adam and Noah were earnest worshipers of Yahweh and were faithful Sabbath keepers (Genesis 6:9, 7:5). They would have taught their descendents about the Bible Sabbath, and its sacredness. The truth that Yahweh is to be worshiped on the seventh of each seven-day week requires a seven-day week, even though they may have later turned to idols and left the worship of the True Elohim.

Let Yahshua Rock Your World

As the descendents of Adam and Noah spread out all over the world, they would have carried with them the seven day week, and the seventh day holy Sabbath given by Yahweh to mankind. Many of Adam's and Noah's descendents became scoffers, however Jones reasoned, that they would still carry with them the twin truths of the Creation Week, of Genesis 1 by their keeping of the seven-day weekly cycle, and the Seventh-day Sabbath by naming the seventh day of the week in their language as the day of Sabbath rest.

Jones decided to research a majority of the languages of the world to see if his reasoning's were true. The results of his research was as he suspected and is another powerful proof, not only that the Seventh day is the true Sabbath of Yahweh, but also that the creation account in Genesis 1 and 2 is accurate, and that Yahweh is our Creator.

Sabbath Around the World

Chart of the Week (Showing the position of the true Sabbath)

LANGUAGE (Where Spoken, Read, or Otherwise Used)	1	2	3	4	5	6	Name of the SEVENTH DAY
Shemitic Hebrew Bible world-wide	Day One	Day Second	Day Third	Day Fourth	Day Fifth	Day the Sixth	Yom hash-shab-bath Day the Sabbath
Hebrew (Ancient and Modern)	One into the Sabbath	Second into the Sabbath	Third into the Sabbath	Fourth into the Sabbath	Fifth into the Sabbath	Eve of Holy Sabbath	Shab-bath Sabbath
Targum of Onkelos (Hebrew Literature)	Day One	Day Second	Day Third	Day Fourth	Day Fifth	Day the Sixth	Yom hash-shab-bath Day the Sabbath
Targum Dialect of the Jews in Kurdistan	Day One of the Seven	Day 2nd of the Seven	Day 3rd of the Seven	Day 4th of the Seven	Day 5th of the Seven	Day of Eve (of Sabbath)	yoy-met sha-bat kodesh Holy Sabbath Day
Ancient Syriac "Each day proceeds on, and belongs to the Sabbath"	One into Sabbath	Two into Sabbath	Three into Sabbath	Four into Sabbath	Five into Sabbath	Eve (of Sabbath)	Shab-ba-tho Sabbath
Chaldee Syriac Kurdistan and Urdmia, Persia	One into Sabbath	Two into Sabbath	Three into Sabbath	Four into Sabbath	Five into Sabbath	Eve (of Sabbath)	Shap-ta Sabbath
Samaritan (Old Hebrew Letters) Nablus, Palestine	Day One	Day Second	Day Third	Day Fourth	Day Fifth	Day Sixth	Shab-bath Sabbath
Babylonian Euphrates & Tigris Valleys Mesopotamia (Written lang. 3800 B.C.)	First	Second	Third	Fourth	Fifth	Sixth	Sa-ba-tu Sabbath
Assyrian Euphrates and Tigris Valleys, Mesopotamia	First	Second	Third	Fourth	Fifth	Sixth	sa-ba-tuSabbath
Arabic (Very old names)	Business Day	Light Moon	War Chief	Turning Day or Midweek	Familiar or Society Day	Eve (of Sabbath)	
Arabic (Ancient and Modern) Western Asia, E,W & North Africa	The One	The Two	The Three	The Four	The Fifth	Assembly (day, Muham)	as-sabt The Sabbath

191

Let Yahshua Rock Your World

Chart of the Week (Showing the position of the true Sabbath)

LANGUAGE (Where Spoken, Read, or Otherwise Used)	1	2	3	4	5	6	Name of the SEVENTH DAY
Maltese Malta	One (day)	Two (and day)	The 3 (3rd day)	The 4 (4th day)	Fifth (day)	Assembly	Is-sibt. The Sabbath
Ge-ez or Ethiopic Abyssinia (Ge-ez signifies "original")	One (day)	Second	Third	Fourth	Fifth	Eve (of Sabbath)	san-bat Sabbath
Tigre Abyssinia (Closely related to Ge-ez)	One (First day)	Second	Third	Fourth	Fifth	Eve (of Sabbath)	san-bat Sabbath
Amharic Abyssinia (Nearly related to Ge-ez)	One	Second	Third	Fourth	Fifth	Eve (of Sabbath)	san-bat Sabbath
Falasha (Language of the Jews of Abyssinia)	One	Second	Third	Fourth	Fifth	Sixth	yini sanbat The Sabbath
Coptic Egypt (A dead language for 200 years)	The First Day	The 2nd Day	The 3rd Day	The 4th Day	The 5th Day	The 6th Day	pi sabboton The Sabbath
Oroma or Galla South of Abyssinia (This language has two sets of names, the first being the oldest)	Lady, Virgin Mary Day. Great or Festival Sabbath	Second day - First Trade Day	3rd Day to the Sabbath - Second Trade Day	4th day to the Sabbath -Fourth (day)	Fifth. (day)	Assembly (day)	Last day of the half-week - inclusive of 4th day Little or Humble or Solemn Sabbath. (A day of no ceremonial display and no work)
Tamashek or Towarek (From ancient Lybian or Numidian). Atlas Mountains, Africa.	First day	Second day	Third day	Fourth day	Fifth day	Assembly Day	a-hal es-sabt The Sabbath Day
Kabyle or Berber (Ancient Numidian) North Africa	Day the One (First)	Day the Two (2nd)	Day the Three (3rd)	Day the Four (4th)	Day the Fifth	The Assembly Day	ghes or wars assebt The Sabbath Day
Hausa (Central Africa)	The One (1st)	The Two (2nd)	The Three (3rd)	The Four (4th)	The Fifth	The Assembly	The Sabbath
Urdu or Hindustani (Muhammadan and Hindu, India) (Two names for the days)	One to Sabbath. Sunday	2nd to Sabbath. Moon-day	3rd to Sabbath. Mars	4th to Sabbath. Mercury	5th to Sabbath. (Eve of Juma)	Assembly (day)	sanichar – Saturn shamba – Sabbath
Pashto or Afghan Afghanistan	One to the Sabbath	Two to Sabbath	Three to Sabbath	Four to Sabbath	Five to Sabbath	Assembly (day)	khali- Unemployed-day, Shamba - Sabbath

Sabbath Around the World

The previous tables include some of the oldest languages known to man. Very few realize that the word "Sabbath" and the concept of resting from work on the seventh day of the week (Saturday) is common to most of the ancient and modern languages of the world. This is evidence totally independent of the Scriptures that confirms the Biblical teaching that Yahweh's Seventh Day Sabbath predates Judaism. The concept of a Saturday holy day of rest was understood, accepted, and practiced by virtually every culture from Babylon through modern times.

In the study of the many languages of mankind you will find two important facts:

1. In the majority of the principal languages the last, or seventh, day of the week is designated as "Sabbath."

2. There is not even one language which designates another day as the "day of rest."

From these facts we may conclude that not only those people who called the last day of the week "Sabbath" but all other peoples and races, as far as they recognized any day of the week as "Sabbath," rested on the seventh day. In fact, it was recorded by the great historian, Socrates, that in his time the whole known world, with the exception of Rome and Alexandria, observed the seventh day of the week.

> "The people of Constantinople, and almost everywhere, assemble together on the Sabbath, as well as on the first day of the week, which custom

Let Yahshua Rock Your World

is never observed at Rome or at Alexandria." Socrates, "Ecclesiastical History," Book 7, chap.19.

Another interesting fact is that the words in the original languages that are used to designate the seventh day of the week as the "Sabbath;" have continued to be very similar while the other words have been so changed over time that they are unintelligible to people of other language groups. This is another proof that the Sabbath and the words used to designate the seventh day of the week as the "Sabbath Day;" originated at Creation in complete harmony with the Biblical record found in Genesis 2:1-3.

Language List		
Language	Word for Saturday / 7thDay	Meaning
Greek	Sabbaton	Sabbath
Latin (Italy)	Sabbatum	Sabbath
Spanish (Spain)	Sabado	Sabbath
Portuguese (Portugal)	Sabbado	Sabbath
Italian (Italy)	Sabbato	Sabbath
French (France)	Samedi	Sabbath day
High German (Germany)	Samstag	Sabbath
Prussian (Prussia)	Sabatico	Sabbath
Russian (Russia)	Subbota	Sabbath
Polish	Sobota	Sabbath
Hebrew	Shabbath	Sabbath
Afaghan	Shamba	Sabbath
Hindustani	Shamba	Sabbath
Persian	Shambin	Sabbath
Arabic	Assabt	The Sabbath
Turkish	Yomessabt	Day Sabbath
Malay	Ari-Sabtu	Day Sabbath
Abyssinian	Sanbat	Sabbath
Lusatian (Saxony)	Sobota	Sabbath

Sabbath Around the World

Language List

Language	Word for Saturday / 7thDay	Meaning
Bohemian	Sobota	Sabbath
Bulgarian (Bulgaria)	Subbota	Sabbath
New Slovenian (Illyria, in Austria)	Sobota	Sabbath
Illyrian (Dalmatia, Servia)	Sobota	Sabbath
Wallachian (Roumania or Wallachia)	Sambata	Sabbath
Roman (Sapin, Catalonia)	Dissapte	Day Sabbath
Ecclesiastical Roman (Italy)	Sabbatum	Sabbath
D'oc. French (ancient and modern)	Dissata	Day Sabbath
Norman French (10th - 11th Centuries)	Sabbedi	Sabbath Day
Wolof (Senegambia, West Africa)	Alere-Asser	Last Day Sabbath
Congo (West Equatorial Africa)	Sabbado or Kiansbula	Sabbath
Orma (South of Abyssiania)	Zam-ba-da	Sabbath
Kazani - TARTAR (East Russia)	Subbota	Sabbath
Osmanlian (Turkey)	Yome-es-sabt	Day of the Sabbath
Arabic (Very old names)	Shi-yar	Chief or rejoicing day
Ancient Syriac	Shab-ba-tho	Sabbath
Chaldee Syriac (Kurdistan, Urumia, Persia)	Shaptu	Sabbath
Babylonian Syriac (A Very Old Language)	Sa-Ba-tu	Sabbath
Maltese (Malta)	Is-sibt	the Sabbath
Ethiopic (Abyssinia)	San-bat	Sabbath
Coptic (Egypt)	Pi sabbaton	the Sabbath
Tamashek (Atlas mountains, Africa)	A-hal es-sabt	the Sabbath
Kabyle (North Africa, Ancient Numidan)	Ghas assebt	the Sabbath day
Hausa (Central Africa)	Assebatu	the Sabbath
Pasto (Afghanistan)	Shamba	Sabbath

Language List

Language	Word for Saturday / 7thDay	Meaning
Pahlivi (ancient Persian)	Shambid	(pleasantest day of the week)
Persian (Persia)	Shambah	Sabbath
Armenian (Armenia)	Shapat	Sabbath
Kurdish (Kurdistan)	Shamba	Sabbath
Ndebele (Zimbabwe)	Sabatha	Sabbath
Shona (Zimbabwe)	Sabata	Sabbath

Miscellaneous Middle Ages Languages		
Georgian (Caucasus)	Shabati	Sabbath
Suanian (Caucasus)	Sammtyn	Sabbath
Ingoush (Caucasus)	Shatt	Sabbath
Malayan (Malaya, Sumatra)	Hari sabtu	day Sabbath
Javanese (Java)	Saptoe or saptu	Sabbath
Dayak (Borneo)	Sabtu	Sabbath
Mandingo (west Africa, s. of Senegal)	Sibiti	Sabbath
Teda (central Africa)	Essebdu	The Sabbath
Bornu (central Africa)	Assebdu	The Sabbath
Logone (central Africa)	Se-sibde	The Sabbath
Bagrimma (central Africa)	Sibbedi	Sabbath
Maba (central Africa)	Sab	Sabbath
Permian (Russian)	Subota	Sabbath
Votiak (Russian)	Subbota	Sabbath

Worf, Jason. "Sabbath Around The World," http://www.sabbathtruth.com/documentation/languages.asp

GRACE

Appendix 6:
GRACE

(The True Meaning)

The word "**Torah**" is translated as "**Law**" in most Bibles. The word "**Torah / Law**" really means "Yahweh's Teachings and Instructions." When we look at the Scriptures in this light, it should take on a whole new meaning when we come to the word "**Law**" in our Bibles.

Most people who sit down to read and / or study the Scriptures do not realize that the Bible is its own dictionary on different terms / words. There is great depth to the Written Word of Almighty Yahweh IF we take the time to search these things out. One MUST want His Truths from His Written Set-Apart (Holy) Word to be able to understand His Divine Message He has given us. I encourage everyone to spend prayerful time every day reading and studying His Word to those who have ears to hear and eyes to see.

> **When you read the Scriptures, you are looking into Yahweh's eyes.**

Let Yahshua Rock Your World

In this Appendix, we are going to do a study on the true Biblical and Scriptural meaning of "**Grace**." We come across this word repeatedly in the Tanakh (Old Covenant) and the Brit Hadasha (Renewed / New Covenant). This is one of the most misunderstood and incorrectly taught words in all of Christianity. It is being touted as the antithesis (direct opposite) to Yahweh's Torah / Law. If Christianity by and large is incorrectly teaching a different "grace" than what the Scriptures teach us, we must ask ourselves how do we reconcile the words of Messiah Yahshua (Christ Jesus) who prayed that we would be sanctified in the Truth?

> Yahshua (Jesus) said in John 17:17: "Set them apart in Your **Truth** – Your Word is **Truth**."

Now we will look at the word "**truth**" to reveal how it is used.

> Psalm 119:43-44: "And do not take away from my mouth The **Word of Truth** entirely, For I have waited for Your right-rulings; That I might **Guard (Keep / Obey / Do) Your Torah** (Yahweh's Teachings and Instructions) continually, forever and ever…"

> Psalm 119:142: "Your Righteousness is righteousness forever, And **Your Torah is Truth**."

> Psalm 119:151: "You are near, O Yahweh, And **all Your Commands are Truth**."

> Psalm 119:160: "The sum of **Your Word is Truth**, And all Your Righteous right-rulings are forever."

GRACE

Psalm 138:2: "**I bow myself** toward Your Set-Apart Hĕkal (Temple), And give thanks to **Your Name** For Your kindness and for **Your Truth**; For **You have made great Your Word, Your Name**, above all."

Malachi 2:6: "**The Torah of Truth** was in His (Yahshua / Jesus) mouth, and unrighteousness (Torahlessness / Lawlessness) was not found on His (Yahshua / Jesus) lips. He walked with Me in peace and straightness, and turned many away from crookedness."

1 Kings 2:3-4: "And guard the Charge of Yahweh your Elohim: to **walk (do) in His Ways**, to guard His laws, His commands, His right-rulings, and His witnesses, **as it is written in the Torah of Mosheh** (Moses), so that you do wisely all that you do and wherever you turn; so that Yahweh does establish His Word which He spoke concerning me, saying, 'If your sons guard their way, to walk (do) before Me in truth with all their heart and with all their being,' saying, 'there is not to cease a man of yours on the throne of Yisra'ĕl (Israel).' "

We see from the above Scriptures that ***Yahweh's Truth is His Torah / Law***. Thus when we look at Yahshua's prayer in John 17:17, it becomes very clear:

Yahshua said in John 17:17: "***Set them apart (make Holy) in Your Truth (keep / do) – Your Word (Torah / Law) is Truth***."

If the Father answered Yahshua's request, then it means we who choose to receive Yahshua as our Messiah will also receive the Torah / Law which in turn sanctifies (makes Holy) us and sets us apart from the world. And what is the Torah / Law? It is the written Set-Apart (Holy) Word. And what is the "Word?" It is Truth. And what is "Truth?" It is the Torah / Law! With this understanding the teachings of Yahshua come alive:

> John 18:37-38: "Then Pilate said to Him, 'You are a Sovereign, then?' Yahshua answered, 'You say it, because I am a Sovereign. For this I was born, and for this <u>I have come into the world, that I should bear witness to The Truth (Torah / Law)</u>. **Everyone who is of the Truth** (Torah / Law) **hears My Voice**.' Pilate said to Him, 'What is truth?' And when he had said this, he went out again to the Yahudim (Jews), and said to them, 'I find no guilt in Him.' "
>
> John 8:31-32: "So Yahshua said to those Yahudim (Jews) who believed Him, 'If you stay in **My Word**, you are truly My taught ones, and you shall know **the Truth**, and **the Truth** shall make you free.' "

GRACE

Did you notice how Yahshua defined the word *"free"* in John 8:32 when He said *"and the Truth (Torah / Law) shall make you free."* Since we know the Torah / Law is Truth then we also know that the Torah / Law observance (doing) is True Freedom; anything else is bondage. This is the opposite of what is being taught in Christianity. This explains Paul's terminology in Galatians 5:1 which is a teaching on John 8:31-32 and Psalm 119:32 and 45.

We must ask ourselves is *"grace"* the antithesis (direct opposite) of the "Torah / Law?" If so, then the above passages are falsehoods. Rather, *"grace"* is synonymous (identical) with the "Torah/Law." **Yahweh's Torah / Law is Yahweh's Grace**. As we look at the word *"grace"* based on Strong's numbering system, it has two biblical expressions in Hebrew, and two in Greek as shown in the next table:

Hebrew	***Chen***, Strong's # 2580 and 2581
Hebrew	***Chesed***, Strong's # 2616 and 2617
Greek	***Charis***, Strong's # 5485 and 5463
Greek	***Eleos***, Strong's # 1653 and 1656

Now we will take a closer look at ***Chen, Chesed, Charis*** and ***Eleos***.

First we will look at the word *"Chen."* *"Chen"* carries with it meanings of, charm, beauty, loveliness, favor, and preciousness. In the Hebrew *Tanakh* (Old Covenant), this appears 70 times. However, out of the 70 times in Hebrew that *"Chen"* appears, it is translated with the English word *"grace"* 39 times in the King James Version, 9 times in the NASB, 8 times in the NIV, 7 times in the RSV, and 12 in the 1901 ASV. Now compare this to

"Chen's" Greek equivalent, the word *"Charis."* From *"Charis"* we get the English word Charismatic. *"Charis"* also carries a similar meaning of charm, beauty, loveliness, favor, and preciousness. Regardless, look at the number of times *"Chen"* in Hebrew and *"Charis"* in Greek, are each translated to the English word *"grace"* in the Old Covenant and the Renewed / New Covenant:

Tanakh (O.T.), **Chen** (Appears 70 times in Hebrew) Number of times **Chen** is translated as *"grace"*	Brit Hadasha (N.T.), **Charis** (Appears 233 times in Greek) Number of times **Charis** is translated as *"grace"*
KJV…………………………39	KJV…………………………131
NASB………………………09	NASB………………………122
NIV…………………………08	NIV…………………………123
RSV…………………………07	RSV…………………………119
ASV (1901)………………12	ASV (1901)………………132

We can see from the table above how infrequent the word *"grace"* is used in the Old Covenant compared to the Renewed / New Covenant. Based on the above table, one can come to an easy conclusion that there is very little *"grace"* in the "Old Covenant" and much more *"grace"* in the "Renewed / New Covenant." Do you see a problem with this? I do. The meaning of the Hebrew *"Chen"* or the Greek *"Charis"* and its English rendering of *"grace"* is being understood in the wrong way! Remember now, *"Chen"* and *"Charis"* both mean charm, beauty, loveliness, favor and preciousness, **but not** *"grace"* in the sense of being liberated through undeserved kindness or mercy. Now let's look at some Scriptures to put this in its proper perspective.

GRACE

Genesis 6:8: "But Noah found **grace** (**Chen or preciousness**) in the eyes of the LORD (Yahweh)" (KJV).

Proverbs 31:30: "**Favour** (**Chen or loveliness**) is deceitful, and beauty is vain: but a woman that feareth the LORD (Yahweh), she shall be praised" (KJV).

Luke 2:52: "And Yahshua increased in wisdom and stature, and in **favour** (**Charis or preciousness**) with Elohim and men."

Acts 2:47: "...praising Elohim and having **favour** (**Charis or loveliness**) with all the people. And the Master added to the assembly those who were being saved, day by day."

One who has received *"Chen"* or *"Charis"* from Yahweh is also shown favor in the sense of Yahweh saying to you, *"You are precious and beautiful in My sight,"* and it is in this sense that you receive His esteem (respect). But now, what we want to talk about is unmerited or undeserved favor in the sense of mercy and kindness when you do not deserve it. This is the true and accurate definition of *"grace"* but it should **not** be explained with the Hebrew *"Chen"* or the Greek *"Charis."*

Now we will take a look at two more words. The Hebrew word *"Chesed"* and the Greek word *"Eleos."*

The Hebrew word *"Chesed"* means undeserved or unmerited favor in the sense of **"grace,"** kindness, pity, and mercy according to Strong's definition. The Hebrew *"Chesed"* appears in the Old Covenant 251 times. This is roughly about five times as much as in the Renewed / New Covenant! *"Chesed's"* equivalent in the Greek is the word *"Eleos."* The Hebrew *"Chesed"* like the Greek *"Eleos"* carries similar meanings of unmerited favor, grace, kindness, pity, and mercy.

Tanakh (O.T.), **Chesed** The number of times **Chesed** is used when it is translated into English using words like favor, mercy, grace, lovingkindness, and compassion: 251 Times	Brit Hadasha (N.T.), **Eleos** The number of times **Eleos** is used when it is translated into the English using words like favor and mercy. 50 Times

Because the Greek word *"Eleos"* is used so few times in the Renewed / New Covenant compared to *"Chesed"* in the Old Covenant, we are given the understanding that there is a huge amount of *"grace"* in the "Old Covenant" and very little *"grace"* in the "Renewed / New Covenant." This is because we are using the proper definition for *"grace"* according to Hebrew and Greek.

Now let's compare the following table which will reveal the numeric use of the English word *"grace,"* representing Hebrew *"Chen"* and Greek *"Charis"* – words having the meaning of charm, beauty, favor, and preciousness:

GRACE

Tanakh (O.T.), **Chen** (Strong's #2580 and 2581): Charm, beauty, favor, and preciousness. Appears 70 times but translated as *"grace"* 39 times.	Brit Hadasha (N.T.), **Charis** (Strong's #5485 and 5463): Charm, beauty, favor, and preciousness. Appears 233 times but translated as *"grace"* 131 times.

The correct definition of *"grace"* in the Old Covenant is being used incorrectly in the Renewed / New Covenant, again, giving us the impression that there is little *"grace"* in the "Old Covenant" and a lot of *"grace"* in the "Renewed / New Covenant." In truth, however, there is exceedingly more *"grace"* in the "Old Covenant" than in the "Renewed / New Covenant." Conversely, there is more *"favor"* and *"preciousness"* in the "Renewed / New Covenant" than in the "Old Covenant." We should ask ourselves WHY? Because Messiah came and brought with Him the charm, beauty, favor, and preciousness of Yahweh's undeserved favor, mercy, and kindness.

For example, if you were going to be executed for a capital crime but someone with authority said, *"I want to show you my charm, beauty, loveliness, favor, and preciousness,"* would you think they were going to free you from your punishment? Maybe. But what if someone with authority definitely said, *"I want to show you my unmerited favor, kindness, and mercy,"* would you think they were going to free you from your punishment? I would think so. You can love someone yet not release them from punishment. This difference in word meanings explains what is happening with

"Chen" in the Hebrew and *"Charis"* in the Greek. Both words are supposed to give the sense of love, and preciousness, **not** unmerited or undeserved favor through mercy.

To further help us, here are the words of David Bivin, Jerusalem Greek and Hebrew scholar:

> "What Christians think of when they read the word **"grace"** is something close to the sense that chesed carries, that is, God's unmerited favor. What they usually **do not** have in mind when they read the English word **"grace"** in the Bible is its ordinary sense of "charm, beauty" ... English versions of Scripture continued to render charis woodenly as **"grace."** Therefore, the reader of the New Covenant encounters a great deal of grace, and because the context usually dictates the sense of **"mercy,"** the Christian reader has come to see **"grace"** primarily in the sense of **"mercy"** rather than in its ordinary English sense of **"charm, loveliness."** "

Now let's look at some passages which will correctly express unmerited favor or mercy using Hebrew and Greek:

> Psalm 23:6: "Surely goodness and **mercy** (**Chesed or unmerited favor**) shall follow me all the days of my life: and I will dwell in the house of the LORD (Yahweh) for ever" (KJV).

> Exodus 33:18-19: "And he (Moses) said, I beseech Thee, shew me Thy Glory. And He (Yahweh) said,

GRACE

I will make all My goodness pass before thee, and I will proclaim the Name of the LORD (Yahweh) before thee; and will be **gracious** (**Chesed or show unmerited favor**) to whom I will be **gracious** (**Chesed or show unmerited favor**), and will shew mercy on whom I will shew mercy" (KJV).

Jeremiah 9:24: "But let him that glorieth (boasts) glory (boast) in this, that he understandeth and knoweth Me, that I am the LORD (Yahweh) which exercise **lovingkindness** (**Chesed or unmerited favor and mercy**), judgment, and righteousness, in the earth: for in these things I delight, saith the LORD (Yahweh)" (KJV).

Matthew 5:7: "Blessed are the **merciful** (**linked to Eleos or undeserved favor**): for they shall obtain **mercy** (**Eleos or undeserved favor and grace**)" (KJV).

Luke 10:36-37: (Yahshua speaking about a Samaritan): "Which now of these three, thinkest thou, was neighbour unto him that fell among the thieves? And He (Yahshua / Jesus) said, He that shewed **mercy** (**Eleos or unmerited favor or grace**) on him. Then said Jesus (Yahshua) unto him, Go, and do thou likewise (the same)" (KJV).

Romans 11:30-31: "For as ye in times past have not believed God (Elohim), yet have now obtained

mercy (**Eleos or unmerited favor**) through their unbelief: Even so have these also now not believed (disobedient), that through Your (Yahweh) **mercy** (**Eleos or unmerited favor**) they also may obtain mercy" (KJV).

"Chesed" or *"Eleos"* is best expressed as the love and depth of compassion a mother has for a child of her womb:

> Isaiah 49:15: "Can a woman forget her sucking child, that she should not have <u>compassion</u> on the son of her womb? yea, they may forget, yet will I not forget thee" (KJV).

In Hebrew it is said *"HaRachaman,"* the Compassionate One, which is linked to ***racham***-Strong's #7355 / 7356 and ***rechem***-*Strong's #7359*. Oftentimes in the Old Covenant, you will see *"**Racham**"* (compassion) and *"**Chesed**"* (mercy or undeserved favor) together:

> Psalm 145:8: "The LORD (Yahweh) is gracious, and full of **compassion** (**rachum**-Strong's #7349); slow to anger, and of great **mercy** (**chesed**-Strong's #2617)" (KJV).

> Psalm 86:15: "But Thou, O Lord (Master), art a God (Elohim) full of **compassion** (**rachum**-Strong's #7349), and gracious, long suffering, and plenteous in **mercy** (**chesed**-Strong's #2617) and truth" (KJV).

GRACE

SUMMARY:

In every place of the Renewed / New Covenant where the English word *"grace"* appears (translated by *Charis*) it should be correctly understood as favor or preciousness according to *"Chen's"* definition. Likewise, where "**mercy**" appears (translated by *Eleos*), it should be correctly understood as unmerited favor according to *"Chesed's"* definition. In other words, *"grace"* in the "Renewed / New Covenant" is wrongly doing the work of *"Chesed"* or "undeserved favor." Rather, it should be doing the work of *"Chen"* or "preciousness." Look at the follow table:

Tanakh (O.T.)	Brit Hadasha (N.T.)
Chesed *(undeserved favor)* 251 times.	**Eleos** *(undeserved favor)* 50 times.
Chen *(preciousness)* 70 times.	**Charis** *(preciousness)* 233 times.

Now we will look at Torah / Law as Grace and Grace as Torah / Law.

Whether *"Chesed"* in Hebrew or *"Eleos"* in Greek, the meaning is unmerited or undeserved favor, mercy, and even lovingkindness. Now, watch how this meaning is connected to the Torah / Law, Yahweh's Torah / Law:

> Psalm 103:11: "For as the heaven is high above the earth, so great is His **mercy** (**chesed or grace**) toward them that fear Him" (KJV).

Let Yahshua Rock Your World

> Psalm 118:4: "Let <u>them now that fear the LORD (Yahweh)</u> say, that His **mercy** (**chesed or grace**) endureth for ever" (KJV).

> Proverbs 16:6: "By **mercy** (**chesed or grace**) and truth iniquity (Torahlessness / Lawlessness) is purged: and <u>by the fear of the LORD (Yahweh)</u> men depart from evil" (KJV).

Yahweh shows us that *"Chesed"* (undeserved favor, mercy, lovingkindness) is connected to those who fear Him. So, naturally we should want to know what it means to fear Yahweh. The answer is easily found in the "words" of Yahweh:

> Deuteronomy 17:19: "And it shall be with him, and he shall read it all the days of his life, so <u>that he learns to fear Yahweh his Elohim and guard (keep / obey / do) all the Words of this Torah and these laws (statutes)</u>, to do them…"

> Deuteronomy 31:12: "Assemble the people, the men and the women and the little ones, and your sojourner who is within your gates, so that they hear, and so <u>that they learn to fear Yahweh your Elohim and guard to do **all** the Words of this Torah.</u>"

In the Old Covenant, to fear Yahweh is to keep His Commandments, and His Commandments are *"Chesed,"* or "**grace**" and "**mercy**" to us. Put another way, **those who receive His** *"Chesed,"* **or** "**grace**" **and** "**mercy,**" **are those who accept Yahweh's Commandments and fear Him.** To those who receive

GRACE

Yahweh's *"Chesed,"* these also receive His *"Chen"* which is favor, and preciousness. This concept explains what is written in John 1:17-18:

> "For the Law (Torah) was given by Moses, *but* **grace** (**Chen—loveliness, favor, preciousness**) and Truth (**Law**) came by Jesus Christ (Yahshua Messiah). No man hath seen God (Elohim) at any time; the only begotten Son, which is in the bosom of the Father, He (Yahshua) hath declared *Him (Yahweh)*" (KJV).

The way most understand this passage is, *"The Torah / Law was given through Moses **but now** we have grace and truth through Yahshua."* **However**, this is incorrect with our improper understanding of *"**grace**"* in the Hebrew and Greek. But, once we correctly translate *"**grace**"* as the precious and lovely words of the Torah / Law, it all falls into place! Now, we have John 1:17-18 saying something like this:

> The Torah / Law was given through Moses and the Torah's / Law's beauty (**Chen**) – loveliness, charm (grace), **and** Truth was realized through the Messiah!

This makes sense in light of the whole counsel of Yahweh's Word!

Now we are going to look at getting Grace.

Yahshua who was the beauty, loveliness, charm, preciousness, and truth of Torah / Law, came to turn all of us back to Yahweh as Peter said in 1 Peter 1:20-21:

> "…foreknown, indeed, before the foundation of the world, but manifested in these last times for your sakes, Who through Him believe in Elohim who raised Him from the dead and gave Him esteem, so that your belief and expectation are in Elohim."

Whether in the Old Covenant or the Renewed / New Covenant, *"mercy"* (undeserved kindness) and *"grace"* (the preciousness and favor of Yahweh) is shown to us, so that we will return to Yahweh and His divine instructions. In Hebrew, it is called **tshuvah**, or repentance; and repentance is always linked to returning to the Torah / Laws of Yahweh:

> 2 Chronicles 30:9: "For if you turn back to Yahweh, your brothers and your children shall be shown compassion by their captors, even to return to this land. For Yahweh your Elohim shows favour and compassion, and does not turn His face from you if you turn back to Him."

When we go back to Yahweh, we always go back to the Torah / Law. So, it's Yahweh's *"**Chesed**"* or undeserved favor, mercy, and lovingkindness that always leads us back to the Torah / Law which in turn directs us to fear Him which in turn leads us to listen to Yahshua who represents Yahweh's *"**Chen**"* (favor and

GRACE

loveliness) and *"**Chesed**"* (mercy and kindness), both which work in partnership with the Torah / Law.

By now, we should have a much clearer understanding of the "**true**" meaning of *"**Grace**"* as clearly defined by Scripture. Scripture is its own best dictionary for the words we read.

Second Timothy 2:15 reads "Do your utmost to present yourself approved to Elohim, a worker who does not need to be ashamed, rightly handling the Word of Truth."

Let Yahshua Rock Your World

> "For you were bought with a price, therefore esteem Elohim in your body and in your spirit, which are of Elohim."
> (1 Corinthians 6:20)

Resources

Books:

Alewine, Hollisa. *The Creation Gospel*

Bailey, Arthur, Apostle, D.Div. *Sunday Is Not The Sabbath?*

ben Mordechai, Avi. *Galatians: A Torah-Based Commentary In First Century Hebrew Context*

Bennett, Todd D. *Walk in the Light: Restoration*

Bennett, Todd D. *Walk in the Light: Names*

Bennett, Todd D. *Walk in the Light: Sabbath*

Bennett, Todd D. *Walk in the Light: Scriptures*

Bennett, Todd D. *Walk in the Light: Covenants*

Bennett, Todd D. *Walk in the Light: The Redeemer*

Bennett, Todd D. *Walk in the Light: The Redeemed*

Bennett, Todd D. *Walk in the Light: Law and Grace*

Chumney, Eddie. *Restoring The Two Houses Of Israel*

Chumney, Eddie. *The Seven Festivals Of The Messiah*

Chumney, Eddie. *Who Is The Bride Of Christ*

Esposito, Don. *The Great Falling Away*

Koenig, William. *Eye To Eye*

Koster, Chris. *Come Out Of Her My People*

Moody, Valarie. *The Feasts of Adonai*

Rives, Richard. *Too Long In The Sun*

White, Lew. *Fossilized Customs*

White, Lew. *In The Twinkling of an Eye – The End of Days*

White, Lew. *Torah Zone*

Willis, Norman. *Nazarene Israel*

Resources

Websites:

www.wildbranch.org
www.elshaddaiministries.us
www.4sephardim.com
www.eliyah.com
www.yrm.org
www.worldnetdaily.com
www.hearoisrael.org
www.intotruth.org
www.hope-of-israel.org
www.hebraiccommunity.org
www.biblicalholidays.com
www.mayimhayim.org
www.betemunah.org
www.israelnet.tv
www.nazarite.net
www.gnmagazine.org
http://lionlamb.net/v3/
www.splitrockresearch.org
www.hebroots.org
www.wisdomintorah.com
www.billcloud.org
www.godslearningchannel.com
www.coyhwh.com
www.fossilizedcustoms.com
www.restorationoftorah.org
www.heartofwisdom.com
www.goodnewsaboutgod.com
www.haydid.org
www.search-the-scriptures.org
www.jerusalemperspective.com
www.wyattmuseum.com
www.theappleofgodseye.com
www.emetministries.com
www.missiontoisrael.org
www.yourarmstoisrael.com
www.sabbathtruth.com
www.menorah.org.za/come_out_of_her_my_people/index.html
www.torahzone.net/anniversarytobah.html
www.thercg.org/articles/abcc.html
www.yrm.org/feasts-forever.htm

References:

Strong's Concordance
World Publisher
ISBN # 0-529-06334-4

Interlinear Bible
Sovereign Grace Publishing or Hendrickson Publishing (same edition by Green)
ISBN # 1-878442-81-1
ISBN # **978-1-56563-977-5** (number for new edition)

Englishman's Greek and Hebrew Concordances
(2 separate volumes) Hendrickson Publisher (Wigram)
Greek ISBN # 0-013573-23-X
Greek ISBN # **978-1-56563-207-3** (number for new edition)
Hebrew ISBN # 1-56563-208-7
Hebrew ISBN # **978-1-56563-208-0** (number for new edition)

Hebrew and Greek Lexicon
Thayer's or Brown, Driver, Briggs-Gesenius
Greek Thayer's ISBN # 0-913573-22-1
Hebrew Gesenius ISBN # 0-913573-20-5

Concordance to the Septuagint
Publisher - Hatch and Redpath
ISBN # 0-8010-2141-3

Etymological Dictionary of Biblical Hebrew
by Matityahu Clark
ISBN # 1-58330-431-2

Resources

Kleins Etymological Dictionary of the Hebrew Language
by Ernst Klein
ISBN # 965-220-093-X

The Ancient Hebrew Lexicon of the Bible
by Jeff A. Benner, VBW Publishing
ISBN # 1-58939-776-2
Visit Dr. Benner's web site at www.ancient-hebrew.org/?

Hebrew Word Pictures
by Dr. Frank Seekins www.livingwordpictures.com/?

Cruden's Compact Concordance
by Alexander Cruden
ISBN # 0-319-48971

> "Remember this, and show yourselves men; turn it back, you transgressors. Remember the former events of old, for I am El, and there is no one else – Elohim, and there is no one like Me, declaring the end from the beginning, and from of old that which has not yet been done, saying, 'My counsel does stand, and all My delight I do…'"
> (Isaiah 46:8-10)

Questions and Answers

Question: Do you love your Creator?
Answer: ☐ **Yes** ☐ **Maybe** ☐ **Sometimes** ☐ **No**

Question: How does He define our love for Him?
Answer: If we keep His Commandments
(John 14:15; 1 John 2:5; 2 John 6)

Question: What does the Scripture mean "walk as He walked" in 1 John 2:6?
Answer: Obey the Torah just as He did: Keep His Sabbaths, Dietary Laws, Feasts Days; and use His True Name

Question: What is the Savior's Hebrew name?
Answer: Yahshua (Yah-shoo-ah)

Question: What is His Father's Hebrew name?
Answer: Yahweh (Yah-way)

Question: If you moved to another country, would your name change?
Answer: No

Question: Why was the Father's Name changed to a pagan deity and His Son's Name changed to titles and a Greek name?

Let Yahshua Rock Your World

Answer: The enemy didn't want the most powerful name in the heavens and the earth to be uttered (Jeremiah 10:6; Acts 4:12)

Question: Who changed His Name?
Answer: The Bible translators – many Bible Prefaces state this fact

Question: What is the New (Re-newed) Covenant?
Answer: Yahweh will put His Law (Torah) within us and write it on our hearts by His Spirit (Jeremiah 31:33)

Question: Who is the New (Re-newed) Covenant with?
Answer: The House of Judah and the House of Israel (Jeremiah 31:31; Hebrews 8:8)

Question: How do we participate in the Re-newed Covenant?
Answer: We have to be grafted in (Romans 11:11-24)

Question: What happens when we are grafted in?
Answer: We become a member of the commonwealth of Israel (Ephesians 2:12-13, 19-22)

Question: What does it mean to worship Him in Spirit and in Truth?
Answer: *Spirit* – Yahshua the living Torah – Brit Hadasha (Renewed / New Covenant)

Truth – Yahshua the written Torah – Tanakh (Old Covenant)

Torah is <u>Truth</u>, but we need the <u>Spirit</u> also to give LIFE to the LETTER

We keep His Commandments (letter) the way He interprets them (Spirit)
(http://www.hoshanarabbah.org/pdfs/spiritandtruth.pdf)

Question: Was our Savior a Christian?

Questions and Answers

Answer: No. He was a Nazarene (Matthew 2:23); and His followers were called Nazarenes (Acts 24:5), and they were also in the "Way" in verse 14. Christianity was not around during the time when Yahshua walked the earth in the flesh. The word "Christianity" cannot be found in any concordance. It is not a religion *practiced* or *started* by Yahshua of Nazareth. We are to graft into His Vine and become fellow citizens of the commonwealth of Israel – partakers of all the promises made to Israel. Even those who are natural born Israelites be they from the tribe of Judah (Jews) or from the other tribes; they to have to be grafted into the commonwealth of Israel to be a citizen of Israel and a child of Yahweh.

Question: What does the word "Law" mean in the Scriptures?
Answer: Torah

Question: What does Torah mean?
Answer: Instructions – "to teach, to point out as aiming the finger"

Question: What is the purpose of Torah?
Answer: It is intended for INSTRUCTION <u>AFTER</u> SALVATION. After we are saved by grace through faith, then the Spirit leads us into all Truth, the Torah, which instructs us how to grow in maturity and please Him.

Question: When the Savior taught His disciples, which Scriptures did He teach from, i.e., Old Covenant or Renewed / New Covenant?
Answer: Old Covenant – the Renewed / New Covenant was not compiled at that time

Let Yahshua Rock Your World

Question: What Scripture was Paul talking about when he said in 2 Timothy 3:16, "All Scripture is given by inspiration of God and is profitable for doctrine, for reproof, for correction, for instruction in righteousness?"
Answer: Old Covenant – the Renewed / New Covenant was not compiled at that time

Question: What is the Forth Commandment?
Answer: Remember the Sabbath to keep it Holy (Set-Apart)

Question: Should we keep the Forth Commandment?
Answer: Yes, nowhere in Scripture was it ever done away with

Question: Can I choose my own day of rest?
Answer: Not if you want to be obedient – He already chose the day for us to rest – the seventh day Sabbath

Question: Who changed the seventh day Sabbath to first day Sunday?
Answer: Constantine – through the Roman Catholic Church

Question: What is the Third Commandment?
Answer: Thou shalt not take the name of the Lord thy God in vain

Question: What does the Third Commandment forbid?
Answer: Taking His Name in vain

Question: What does "vain" mean?
Answer: Strong's Concordance #7723 – "Make desolate or bring to ruin, uselessness, emptiness, nothingness." When you do not speak His Set-Apart Name, you are bringing His Name to ruin, nothingness.

Question: What are the three major pagan traditions in the Church?
Answer: Christmas, Easter, and Sunday worship

Questions and Answers

Question: Which Church is Elohim's true Church?
Answer: The one that keeps His Commandments in the Spirit of Truth

Question: Should Christians celebrate the Feast of "Passover"?
Answer: Yes and we will keep it during His Kingdom reign (Matthew 26:29)

Question: Has the Feast of Tabernacles been done away with?
Answer: No. It's mentioned in the Book of Revelation as a future event (Revelation 21:3; Zechariah 14:16)

Question: Was the Savior crucified on Good Friday?
Answer: No, He was crucified on Wednesday evening

Question: Did He rise up on Easter Sunday?
Answer: No, He rose at the end of the Sabbath

Question: Will the Sabbath exist in the future?
Answer: Yes, time is reckoned from Sabbath to Sabbath in the future (Hebrews 4:9; Isaiah 66:22-23)

Question: What is Syncretism?
Answer: Mixture

Question: Is Christmas in the Bible?
Answer: No, it's a man-made holiday based on pagan customs (Jeremiah 10:1-5)

Question: Are the Feasts mentioned in Leviticus 23 for the Yahudim (Jews), for Christians, or both?
Answer: They are for everyone who wants to please Him and walk as He walked

Question: What is the mark of the Covenant that shows we belong to Him?
Answer: The Sabbath

Let Yahshua Rock Your World

Question: What did the Savior mean when He said, "Let the dead bury the dead" in Matthew 8:22?
Answer: It's a Hebrew idiom referring to the "second burial" system practiced at that time

Question: Should we keep His Commandments?
Answer: Absolutely!

Question: How many of His Commandments should we keep?
Answer: All ten of them

Question: Who founded Christianity?
Answer: The Roman Catholic Church

Question: What is the Creator's religion?
Answer: It was called "The Way" (Ironically, He is the Way, the Truth and the Life)

Question: Who is the Bride?
Answer: Those who follow Torah, are washed with the water of the Word, and come to spiritual maturity without blemish (Ephesians 5:26-27)

Question: Who will enter Yahweh's Holy City?
Answer: Those who <u>do</u> His Commandments (Revelation 22:14)

Question: What is the Greatest Commandment?
Answer: To love Yahweh with all our heart, soul, mind and strength (Matthew 22:36-38)

Question: How do we love Him that way?
Answer: Obey Him by KEEPING HIS COMMANDMENTS!

www.ingramcontent.com/pod-product-compliance
Lightning Source LLC
Chambersburg PA
CBHW061256110426
42742CB00012BA/1946